USUAL

The Rants and I
of a Psychoth.

Geoffrey Windham

USUAL ME

The Rants and Ramblings of a Psychotherapist

Geoffrey Windham

PS AVALON
Glastonbury, England

© Geoffrey Windham 2007

First published in the U.K. in 2007 by PS Avalon

PS Avalon
Box 1865, Glastonbury
Somerset, BA6 8YR, U.K.
www.psavalon.com

Geoffrey Windham asserts the moral right
to be identified as the author of this work

Front Cover Illustration: Willi Gray

Back Cover Photo: Carole Windham

Design: Will Parfitt

All rights reserved. No part of this publication may be reproduced, sorted in a retrieval system, or transmitted in any form or by any means, electronic, mechanical, photocopying, recording or otherwise, without the prior permission of the publisher, except in the case of brief quotations embodied in articles and reviews.

ISBN 978-0-9552786-2-4

Contents

About the Author		6
Dedications		7
Introduction		8
One	Identities	11
Two	Usual Me	15
Three	A Context for Therapy	17
Four	Answering Questions	25
Five	Joining In	30
Six	I Want My Medal	36
Seven	Making Movies	44
Eight	Risk	48
Nine	Sex	59
Ten	Permission Granted	65
Eleven	Attention	69
Twelve	Preference and Commitment	74
Thirteen	Death	78
Fourteen	Singing the Glory of Forms	83
Fifteen	Believing	91
Bibliography		96
Contacting the Author		98
Index		100

About the Author

I have been a therapist for over 15 years, but my experience dates back much earlier than that. I became interested in therapy in the late 1970s and participated in many groups, including the est training.

In 1982 I, my wife Carole, and my daughter Heidi, moved to California partly because of our friends Jenny O'Connor and Russell Rae. Jenny was a psychic channel and resident teacher at Esalen Institute, Big Sur. We took part in experiential trainings there and we were lucky enough to meet Dick Price, Janet Zuckerman, Freddy Boeve, Janet Lederman, Bette Dingman and Betty Fuller. Esalen was the original centre in America for new directions in therapy and consciousness. Many conferences and workshops have been held there over the years.

We returned to England in 1986 and I began to take formal training. In the early 90s I gained valuable experience as a nurse on an acute admission ward in a psychiatric hospital. I learned a lot from the patients. Then I worked at a drug and alcohol agency counselling people with various forms of addictions.

In 1994 I was employed as a counsellor at the University of East London in the student services department. This gave me the opportunity to be with people from cultures and countries all over the world.

I now work in private practice, as well as presenting groups, seminars and workshops for therapists and organisations with my daughter.

Dedicated with love and kisses to

Carole, *for everything,*
and to my lovelies, Heidi, Spencer, Tegan and Kaden.

Acknowledgements

With all my love to my Mum and Dad, Rosie and Hans; to my Grandparents Celia and David; to my German family who I never had the chance to meet, Gustav, Paula, Elsa, and Oscar; to my sibs, Stephen, Paul and Susan; to all my nieces and nephews, and in memory of my sister Alice who never made it here.

Thank you to Rev. Moshe Glazier for his generosity of spirit; to Jenny O'Connor, Russell Rae and Darryl McDowell for their fierce and tender love; to the Nine, whoever you are; to Arcadia Mel de Fontenay Bandini for her hospitality; to Teddy Lyon for her groundedness; to Sherry Klug for her nerve; to the gestaltists at Esalen, especially Dick Price and Janet Zuckerman, for showing me the possibilities by example; to Werner Erhard for his inspirational use of language; to Dave Jones, my long time supervisor, for his sense of fun allied with serious clinical experience; to Mark Foster for his irreverence; to Chazan Copperman, Rock and Roll, and the Blues for fertilising the musical seed my Mum planted in me; to Phil and Willi Gray for their support and friendship; and to Rachael Clyne for being my lifelong friend and ushering me into places I would not have visited.

Thank you to all the people who have allowed me to share in their lives, in their pains and sorrows, their joys and achievements, and for helping me to realise the Geoffreyness that I am and I am not.

Introduction

This book is about my way of being a therapist, and some of my beliefs and assumptions about what it means to be a human being. This is based solely and subjectively on Geoffrey Windham, the human I know best. Geoffrey is not equipped to tell the truth, the whole truth and nothing but the truth.

I have often discussed what I should bring to therapy: boundaries, theories, training, experience, and the words and ideas I have read in the books and articles I proudly display on my bookshelves, but all I can bring is my version of all this, my peculiar distortion of reality. Whatever intervention I make, whatever model I believe I am following, however elegant or clumsy I may be, it is Geoffrey in relation with another.

Sometimes a person needs stopping, sometimes starting. Sometimes a person needs warming up, sometimes cooling down, sometimes to be excited, sometimes to be calmed, sometimes to be tickled, and sometimes poked. Some people need space, some closeness. Some need to learn to laugh, some to remember how to cry. Some need to learn to forgive, some need to be forgiven.

As well as hopefully discovering their patterns, and how they connect, and possibly to share that with my client, it is my job, as the therapist, to take care of the boundaries, to ensure they are known and transparent, to pay attention to their creation and maintenance, and to be as aware as I can be as to the when and how of both our desires to break and stretch them.

Within this construction, I feel able to comment, silently and out loud, on the boundary's ebb and flow. I also feel able to comment on our way of being and behaviour, our physical, mental, emotional and spiritual demeanour, both the process and the content, as we too ebb away and flow towards each other. Most importantly, I feel able to not know.

Comments are intended to be clearly from where I am, encouraging the other person to comment on the world from their usual perspective, at the same time as knowing that there are other valid positions.

As we notice this, our definitions of self become apparent as a part of our relationship, not just at the boundary, at the edge, but in relation to the other. Two ends need a middle, a place not just to meet but to share. We can both notice this, but sometimes it takes a while to be translated by the brain into speech.

Can we recognise each other and ourselves as embodied human beings, fearful of our mortality, wary of each other, connected and defined by otherness?

Sharing and even celebrating the commonality of our humanity moves both of us through the familiar towards what we already knew but did not dare to admit. This is where the parallel lines meet, a by-product of speaking the language of intimacy.

Gathering Reflections

I gather my reflections
To see who I'm supposed to be
I wrap my human stories round
The nothing in the middle of me.
Dear everybody, how are you all?
And do you really know me well?
You are the planets and the stars orbiting my life
Each one with our own tale to tell

Every little thing I do shows who I am
And a lot of a little is a lot
All the ghosts and the spirits of the future past
Keep reminding me of what I've got.
Is there a practical guide to life on planet earth?
Is there a point, a grand design, is there some goal?
A million billion bodies are miraculously here
Each one a faint mirror image of the whole

It's free here
But there's a life to pay
And time demands
It won't be any other way.
When the price seems too high
Like the plant is in the seed
Find your life within your soul
In that moment you'll be freed

Chapter One • Identities

Who is it?
It's only me.
Which me?
Which one of the multitude of contenders?
One of the mes that is me over here?
One of the mes that is you over there?
Usual mes rule the world that can be ruled.
We rule
by force,
by allowance,
by persuasion,
by temptation,
with love,
with fear,
with whatever works.

When I woke today I knew exactly how to be Geoffrey. I knew what Geoffrey does in the morning, what he has for breakfast, how he brushes his teeth, which shoe he puts on first. I knew the kinds of clothes he prefers to wear, what language he speaks and the kind of internal conversations he has with himself as well as the kinds of conversations he has with others.

In other words, I knew all Geoffrey's preferences, habits and routines. His well practised ways are rooted in genetic inheritance and physical body type, but mostly based on second hand bits of behaviour that he copied and adapted from others along the way for what seemed like a good reason at the time, usually with some survival value. Geoffrey is an expert at Geoffreyness.

Geoffrey's hopes and fears, his dreams and anxieties, his physical postures, his emotional attitudes, and his deeply held principles, are all set and in place, ready to be activated in reaction to the events of the day.

I call the conglomeration of these identity fragments "usual me". A whole made of parts is about as holistic as I can conceive. Usual me includes definitions such as ego, id and superego, adult, parent and child, and the gestalt topdog and underdog duality.

Usual me judges itself, its own identities, on a spectrum from real to false. Usual me judges the faces it shows to the world as false pretences masking the "real" identity which must not be shown. This is like an echo of its purpose. It is not whether these usual me identities are false or real as usual me would like us to believe, but how usual me distracts itself from enquiring as to who it is creating them. I call this who "true me".

Usual me tries to analyse and define everything including true me. True me includes Ken's transpersonal levels of consciousness, such as centaur, subtle and causal.

True me is not an identity. Usual me *is* identity, the physical manifestation of true me. Usual me's job is to be like a shock absorber, to buffer true me from involvement in everyday life. Usual me's strategy to achieve this is to be the centre of its own attention.

It is like a computer having to put all its attention into solving an insoluble problem, with hardly any attention left for anything else. The other side of this is that when usual me is involved in this way and not looking, so to speak, it is possible to quietly slip away from the usual me world. This is how a mantra works.

Usual me is the way we relate in what Martin Buber named the I It world. In it world, usual me is a contracted object or event in a world of contracted objects and events, defined by what usual me is not. Usual me is a local phenomenon, measurable in time and space. Although we may be in close proximity geographically, we do not make personal contact, we are remote.

We may be familiar but we are not intimate. We are alienated by fear from each other and from the world, individually and in our various groupings. My experience of you, is my interpretation of you, is my objectification of you.

How I imagine you experience, interpret and objectify me, and how I want you to experience, interpret and objectify me, affects how I experience myself. Usual me is defined and connected by otherness.

Usual me ways are familiar to us, whatever level of society we occupy. We may feel helpless to be personally different or to make a real difference. Many of us feel the victim of somebody or something, or the one to blame. We are not good enough, famous or successful enough, resentful we are on the outside looking in, or wanting to be on the outside looking in. We may even be too famous or too successful.

There is an assortment of positions in the usual me game and many variations. Perpetrator can seem like the power position. Victim can seem like the weak place, with survivor position an endless getting better. Bystanders can appear to be helpless innocents. All need each other and a particular spin on the past, so they can continue to be the effect of a cause on which they base themselves.

Some positions can be fun, even joyous, but they are based on discrimination, comparison, judgement and prejudice. They are selfish and survival oriented. All can play guilty, shameful, depressed, justified, righteous, humorous, enlightened, self actualised, cool, etc.

Usual me wants the security of the idea that there is a permanent usual me experiencing all this, so it creates the illusion of a thinker that thinks each thought. The cessation of "thinking", which is actually only talking to myself, is also the end of all these thinkers.

This is not achieved by amputation, but by the usual mind knowing itself for what it is, a limitation. Then perhaps the true mind, the still small voice not based on self importance, can be heard.

In this sense, the limited inner talk, the incessant quacking of usual me, based on the known and its projection into the future, is just like surface noise, the scratches of repetition, and of no significance. Nevertheless, we attach so much importance to this noise, acting as if it were composed of commands from some deity that have to be obeyed, resisted, understood, analysed, redirected or reframed. How can a mind like this ever receive anything new?

What is truly new is not an extension of the known or a repetition. For the new to be created there must be a space for it to appear in and the usual mind is all full up of itself.

Trying to empty the usual me mind involves the use of force, which only succeeds in cramming in even more stuff for the usual mind to juggle. So it is not about creating space in a place where space is interpreted into more usual mind stuff; time, distance and comparison. Usual me mind must get that it is the physical manifestation of that space. There is no secret, usual me points directly to true me.

◆

Chapter Two • Usual Me

Usual me is made for and of survival.
Trying to banish the certainty of its death,
It is a sentinel that has become a despot.
It wants and fears to last forever.

What usual me thinks is feeling is not feeling,
it is thinking about feeling.
What usual me thinks is thinking is not thinking,
it is the sound of usual me describing itself and its world to itself,
Keeping up appearances,
Quack, quack, quack.
Yap, yap, yap.

In clock world,
the world of measurement,
usual me is essential to do the comparing,
It tells itself
Who I am,
What I do,
How to tie my shoe laces.
It gives my life meaning and continuity.

Usual me cannot conceive
the reality of the inconceivable,
Cannot see the shadowless, colourless light,
Cannot hear the soundless silent melody,
Must define something to know it,
Must interpret to understand,
and is therefore partial,
A fragment seeking wholeness.

Backstage of usual me posturing.
Usual me must create its own demise
by speaking the language of intimacy,
by cherishing itself.

Laughing at itself,
Ceasing to set this against that
Usual me pauses,
Senses are one,
The usual world stops,
and usual me
vanishes like smoke into an endless sky.

True me is of the unknown
and is free from conditions.
True me is not subject to any objects,
True me is the boundless source of energy,
that permeates any barrier,
transforms any impasse
in the crucible of everyday life.
The glow of this energy is called love.

Chapter Three • A Context for Therapy

I ask myself,
"Am I going crazy?"
I feel like I'm bursting into flame,
My soul whispers,
"Maybe, it's alright, you can love again"
My body is falling,
I'm ready to turn around,
I'm ready to fly my wings,
I'm ready to kiss the ground.

Our hopes of getting better or happier seem to be limited to repeating the popular and fashionable affirmations of personal growth: taking responsibility, owning experience, knowing who we are, letting go. Then there is praying to and following something, trying to transcend something, finding some meaning or being ok with meaninglessness, working out some way to love ourselves, and an ever increasing number of spiritual practices and teachers to follow.

Likewise, an ever expanding body of research insinuates the sorts of things we are supposed to be thinking about, like measurable outcomes and objectively provable justifications for a course of action. We should, we must, organisations and individuals, be able to change and grow, which naturally means to improve. These days, growth means ever more, even the thought of decay is not allowed. There is no notion that decay is a natural part of the cycle, but when the shadow is repressed we all suffer the consequences.

If we do not grow it proves that there is something wrong with us, that we are just not working hard enough, not eating the right foods, not wearing the right clothes, not saying the right words in the right ways, not believing the true beliefs or even consuming enough.

Is it possible, or desirable, to pursue the path of self actualisation or growth whether economically, politically, socially, spiritually, emotionally, mentally, on our own as individuals or as exclusive groups?

Is it selfish to do this and therefore inimical to actualisation? Is it a blind alley that ignores the real problems of our species; that most of us live and die in poverty and its consequences, and yet in therapy the client is supposed to work out feelings about these issues "inside" themselves? We must not decay. Others, not in our club, they can decay for us. They suffer for us as we deny the shadow in ourselves.

Growing can only be defined by what is not growing and so is goal oriented, individualistic and competitive, a usual me activity.

As a western person, with a Jewish background, I was brought up to believe I had the right to be special, that if I wanted something badly enough and worked hard enough, it would eventually come to pass. Family was always important, as was community, but still in an exclusive way, us and them. What the family believed was what I believed and unquestionably real.

Our religious beliefs, within the context of being chosen, were valuable, and by association we were valuable. I had a secure base. We were best in sector. I understood what it meant to feel right.

Later, I became interested in other religions and realised that the nature of religion is about being chosen and others not. The chosen is defined by the unchosen. Being chosen or having a direct line to God or the Devil is about as special as you can be.

The problem with this is in the tension between my individual dream of being a chosen one, one who knows, one who has made it, a member of the club of chosen ones, and my other dream of living in a world that we all share without hunger and poverty.

Religion is about what should be, what is is damned. Living up to what should be is one of our worst self imposed curses. Living up to what should be allows me to judge you as I judge myself and commit dreadful acts.

It is obvious that the spread of religion of whatever type and its politicisation is, together with climate change and the limited supply of oil, gas and fresh water, one of the great threats that we face today. This is not just about what religion preaches or stands for, but the people that are attracted to it.

Many are relatively moderate craving certainty, the need to belong, and some meaning to life, but the celebrities in charge must be hard line, they must appeal to the fanatics, for it is the fanatics that provide the energy to maintain the religion through time.

The religion must be as eternal as the God. The fanatics are the ones who know that they are on the side of God and there seems to be more of them lately. They demand that God be prejudicial. They know that their God and prophets are the true God and prophets, and therefore they have licence to kill and torture those who do not believe, for the good of the world and the good of their souls. At the very least the unbelievers will not make it into heaven.

Lenny Bruce on how religious wars have and continue to be eternal,

> "... a Jew, in the dictionary, is one who is descended from the ancient tribes of Judea... That's what it says in the dictionary, but you and I know what a Jew is: One Who Killed Our Lord... there should be a statute of limitations for that crime..."

Part of the identity of the Christian religion is to blame individual Jews for their messiah's death. How could they possibly let go of that? No Judas no Jesus. It is a component of the vehicle that has driven the religion through time to now, so there is little hope of forgiveness.

Religions thrive on making other religions wrong how ever much they pretend otherwise. Religions do us and them. Even factions within religions war with each other, Protestants and Catholics, Sunnis and Shi'as.

There is no possibility of change because what God wants has been and is being revealed to them, debate is banned. The power of religion to divide continues. It never went away.

The current religious wars are just the modern expression of wars that have been fought for centuries in the name of God. This God was beautifully summed up by Bob Dylan, singing about God's relationship with Abraham, patriarch of Jews, Christians and Muslims.

> "Oh God said to Abraham, "Kill me a son"
> Abe says, "Man, you must be puttin' me on"
> God say, "No."
> Abe say, "What?"
> God say, "You can do what you want Abe, but
> the next time you see me comin' you better run"

Well Abe says, "Where do you want this killin' done?"
God says. "Out on Highway 61".

I could never understand why an omniscient God would want or need to be worshipped, praised and sacrificed to, threatening people into it, killing them if they dared to worship other Gods. This God does not like to be ignored. For our part, we are frightened of being alone, of there being no reason.

The Bible is full of stories of God killing unbelievers and dissenters himself, and giving license to his believers to kill the enemy and rape their women. What kind of basis is this for three of the world's major religions?

It is the same in the Hindu holy book, the Bhagavad-Gita. Arjuna, on the battlefield, has doubts over fighting with and probably killing friends, relatives and teachers. Krishna appears to him and gives him a list of reasons why he should fight, including allowing Arjuna to experience himself as universal consciousness, and telling him that must fight to fulfil his karma. Maybe it is a teaching about the impermanence and unreality of this little life, but I want us to respect our little lives.

The effects on us all of this violent kind of teaching has been disastrous. We have concentrated on the violence rather than the teaching. How many have been killed and tortured in various Gods' names over the centuries? Even now we are suffering for this. Maybe in the bigger picture none of our suffering matters but it matters now, it matters to me.

I love this parody of prayer to such a God from Monty Python's movie The Meaning of Life.

> "Chaplain, Let us praise God. O Lord…
> Congregation, O Lord…
> Chaplain, …ooh, You are so big…
> Congregation, …ooh, You are so big…

Chaplain, ...so absolutely huge.
Congregation, ...so absolutely huge.
Chaplain, Gosh, we're all really impressed down here, I can tell You.
Congregation, Gosh, we're all really impressed down here, I can tell You.
Chaplain, Forgive us, O Lord, for this, our dreadful toadying, and...
Congregation, ...and barefaced flattery.
Chaplain, But You're so strong and, well, so ...super.
Congregation, Fantastic!
Chaplain, Amen.
Congregation, Amen."

A lot of Gods, Goddesses, and people seem to need and demand this kind of narcissistic praising. It seems that this God, as many, can be bought off with worship, sacrifice and a strict adherence to numerous rules.

Then in the Buddhist teaching called the Diamond Sutra, in the section titled, "The Real Teaching of the Great Way", I read with astonishment,

"Buddha said, All the Bodhisattva-Heroes should discipline their thoughts as follows: All living creatures of whatever class, born from eggs, from wombs, from moisture, or by transformation, whether with form or without form, whether in a state of thinking or exempt from thought-necessity, or wholly beyond all thought realms – all these are caused by Me to attain Unbounded Liberation Nirvana. Yet when vast, unaccountable, immeasurable numbers of beings have thus been liberated, verily no being has been liberated.

It is because no Bodhisattva who is a real Bodhisattva cherishes the idea of an ego-entity, a personality, a being, or a separated individuality."

This is one of the greatest jokes ever told. Just thinking about it does strange things to my mind. It took me a while to get it, but I really think it was meant to be humorous, especially so for today when there are so many of us on the planet, and being an individual is such an imperative.

Great teachers use humour. I free all these classes of exotic life from life and death, and yet no one is freed because there was no one to be enslaved in the first place. In fact, there is no first place either. This is also while trying to imagine what "wholly beyond all thought realms" might possibly be like.

These teachings advocate that there is no self and no not self, the unreality of phenomenal distinctions, and that enlightenment is enlightenment because it is nothing special.

However, in the practical everyday world, which may very well be a fleeting dream, if I do not pay my taxes by the due by date, the Inland Revenue will not be interested in the argument that there is no individual to pay them. The renunciate needs a householder from whom he can beg. Try telling someone being tortured or raped that their suffering is not real as they are mistaken about being an individual, sounds good in theory, as a should.

In true me world, I am not an object among objects defined by what usual me is not. I am not the effect of some cause. I am expanded being, not a contracted doing. The problem with this is that meaning and measurement go together.

Meaning is definition, comparison. When all is one, everything is nothing and meaning itself loses its meaning, for there is no-one experiencing anything, no subject experiencing an object, no object to be experienced.

In therapy, awareness and choice have been sold almost as a panacea, but the meaninglessness of it is not part of the sell.

As usual me realises that my version of the usual me world is constructed by me and my relationship with it, usual me also realises that without that construction of mine, my world is devoid of meaning, me too. This can be shocking, depressing, and frightening and can increase my anxiety. Realising my power to choose also makes usual me anxious. Clients intuit this in their avoidance of awareness and choice.

I am contracted in time and space in the usual me world. Usual me needs measurement and predictability, limited choice, to give meaning to my life. Measurement is also a product of the experience of me as other.

The space between me and me as other is the movement of time. Without memory of another me as past, and an idea of another me in the future, I would exist in the present in a very restricted way. The here and now is where I exist but without a measurable and meaningful continuum I would be trapped, unable to act at all. An identity that existed in short, discrete bursts would be almost useless.

Usual me's anxiety is in the realisation that it is itself an act, a familiar and well rehearsed routine, and that the assumption of the other, be it subject or object, is the basic split that self awareness relies on. Self cannot exist without other, self is relationship. Otherness is our gift to God.

As we conform to our groups, whether they are business or education, religious or secular, large or small, tribal or individual, and as we pursue the current definitions of success, the possibility of creating meaning is lost because what I am really conforming to is the groups' meanings and values. Rebelling against that only confirms it.

◆

Chapter Four • Answering Questions

Usual me does not know:
if there is a self or not;
if self perpetuating actualisation or enlightenment is possible;
if having actualisation as a goal is self defeating;
if the conditioned mind, which is conditioning, can uncondition itself;
what, if anything, is being actualised or transcended;
if the life events that seemingly frustrate or distort this progression are somehow a part of the process itself;
if the idea of an individual self is an unchosen, accidental, non goal oriented, genetic attempt at immortality;
if all that I know, all that I feel, all that I think, all that I am, is the effect of chemicals sweeping through the cells of my body;
if this is just a virtual reality, one of many simulations being run on some super computer in the future;
if reincarnation happens and, if it does, whether it is linear in time, or parallel in the sense that an oversoul manifests as multiple and simultaneous incarnations, and that the different lives affect each other karmically right now;
if the usual me mind is a foreign installation, and if we are food for predators that feed on our awareness, and whether I can rebuild my awareness in such a way that it is not palatable;
if the basis for my need to make and break boundaries is acting out my fear of death and of undeath, the end of me, the end of you to me,

the curse of only me to listen to or to think about, being totally alone forever, or just being snuffed out.

Another position comes from my reading of Victor Frankl. The people who survived best in the Nazi concentration camps were the ones who were able to respond individually to the questions that were being asked of them, when one of the purposes of camp life was to completely remove any vestige of individuality from the prisoners.

Frankl wrote,

"What was really needed was a fundamental change in our attitude to life. We had to learn ... it really did not matter what we expected from life, but rather what life expected from us. We needed to stop asking about the meaning of life, and instead to think of ourselves as those who were being questioned by life – daily and hourly. Our answer must consist, not in talk and meditation, but in right action and right conduct. Life ultimately means taking the responsibility to find the right answer to its problems and to fulfil the tasks which it constantly sets for each individual ... his unique opportunity lies in the way he bears his burden."

"... taking responsibility to find the right answer ... the way he bears his burden."

Here is the meaning of acting without want of reward, learning how to listen to the world and how to respond, being able to improvise because life really depends on it. This is being an individual while not trying to stand out in any way, a lightness of touch like Kung Fu's Shaolin monk, Grasshopper, walking on rice paper and making no mark.

Sometimes the current task is suffering, something none of us escapes, but a life based on mourning, regret, and pre-grieving for future losses, fuels a giving-away of energy to what we are the victim of or surviving, and as we survive so does what we are surviving from, both ways.

We go through the motions of being here, but we avoid being here because we know this is where death happens. Here and now is where and when actual pain and suffering occur, not the fantasy versions. Here and now is where and when love and joy occur, not the fantasy versions, but the fear of pain and suffering happening again is often too great to take the risk.

We try to escape from here by trapping ourselves in bubbles of time, fascinating ourselves with trauma, leaking life force by maintaining the bubbles and our attachments to them by acting them out in the present, and projecting them into the future, the roots of revenge. We also maintain these bubbles as storage units in the hope of future completion of the past unfinished business the bubbles contain.

Sometimes an event breaks through our usual defences and we realise we are not invulnerable. We then become fascinated with how this happened, how we were touched by "reality", how to make it happen again if we judge it as positive, how to avoid it if negative.

As long as I avoid, I am attached to what I am avoiding. Negative flashbacks seem to be more attractive, both in content and in the way I hold that content. It's like slowing down to get a good look at an accident on the motorway.

Occasionally, the usual me is so affected by intense emotion such as fear or embarrassment or love, that it temporarily contracts so much that true mind enters the world minus its outer shell. This revelation can be like the clouds parting and the sun shining through or the darkest nightmare. Although usual mind is ruthless in its survival manoeuvres, it is sensitive to criticism and easily wounded. Because of this usual me itself needs protecting.

I believe this is achieved by living the kind of life that Frankl suggested, that is in right action and right conduct.

My actions, what I actually do, these are my little dances with life, the way I respond. This is not a moral point of view but a practical approach. It means acting in ways that reduce usual me's vanity and enhance its humility, facing up to my own mortality. Of all things to take impersonally death is the big one. Death happens to us all. Death is both personal and not personal.

One day, when my death arrives, none of my little tricks will work. Even if usual me has the time to try to talk my way out of it using all the techniques I know, Geoffrey is destined to die.

Usual me may well be formed by an ongoing violent reaction to mother's body or by an incomplete working through of oedipal issues, but by attempting to transcend, escape from or overpower the predicament of being mortal, and the fear and shame of only ever being Geoffrey forever, usual me continues to be a criminal accomplice repeating the insults of the past, rotting and poisoning life.

Keeping the unwanted separate, at a distance, helps us to survive at the time, but also creates the experience as a part, another me. These parts are variations of the violence as we remember experiencing it.

I can switch position between being the victim and the perpetrator, or anyone or anything else associated, be it mother, murderer, non organic object, one of the classes of Buddha's list of life, anything and nothing. Power to control is the supposed attraction and prize. Then the embodied person distorts as we relate to the insults, trying to fit to a misinterpreted understanding of the past, pretending we do not know that it is avoidance.

If we have the energy left, we attempt to pass our pain on in some way, hurting others, getting them to hurt us, pretending that the pain is not there, calling it something else, getting someone else to call it something else, setting targets, blowing people up in the name of God. We treat the world, and that includes self and others, as if it were already dead, something to be used; a thing to be consumed.

We suffer from consumption disorder, the enormous self absorption usual me has with its own doings, which takes all of our attention, and all of our time. Usual me is composed of surrender to whatever authority we depend on for material rewards, approval, reputation, and identity.

Usual me looks for the angle and seeks the advantage. Usual me speaks and understands usual me language, the language of the predator. We are taught this language, sometimes by force masquerading as love, or the need to survive, and in speaking this tongue, we compromise our integrity. We have all been compromised, therapists too. Are therapists just facilitating people to conform to a society which has obviously gone mad with greed, vanity and religious violence?

Chapter Five • Joining In

The sunset glows,
Or is it dawn?
A generation is reborn,
And when the monsters have all gone,
Who's left to know just which one won?

We dress our clients' wounds, even help to heal them, and then send them back to the front line. And how do we not do that? Do we help to make them discontent enough to actually do something? Is it possible to teach the language of right conduct and right action in a world that is seemingly indifferent to us, a mirror for our neglected souls? Drop a baby out of the window, does the ground soften? Or is this not a therapist's concern?

What is needs changing sometimes. We should not collude with a society that deifies vanity, shallowness and celebrity and actively propagates inequality while promising utopia if we wouldn't mind working harder and longer. We know all this, but we do not pay enough attention to the part of us that tells us. Usual me tries to ban such thinking by drowning it out with the noise and repetition of attractive fantasies.

This is just the latest version of a slave society, and we know it, but we look the other way, which means looking out for number one, and that includes success, righteousness, searching for enlightenment or personal growth or pleasure, wishing to sit at God's right hand, (the left just wouldn't be good enough), even desiring to be the last enlightened one into heaven, which presupposes an individual.

We are impoverished because of what we are doing and allowing to be done for our personal gain, and what usual me believes would be too great and simple a truth to bear. This burden is reaction to the reality of death, and its sibling, the truth of what we do, and have done, to each other. Do you really think that we are not affected by what is going on in the world right now? This last few thousand years?

Those that search for scraps in the garbage and for grains of rice in the dust, the homeless, the hungry, the dispossessed and the tortured, and those that perpetrate this, enable us to worship in the malls and feast at the table of too much.

Usual me shakes our heads at today's terrible story in the news, may even give charity and then we get on with our day, buying more stuff to surround ourselves with the symbols of success, and then wondering why we are strangely dissatisfied. We have forgotten that the human race is an entity.

Paradoxically, tragically, in trying to avoid death we live in it. We make ourselves dead as we try to live in this dead world we have created by removing soul from our environment and by splitting into inner and outer, us and them, higher and lower.

I remember when I first realised that royals were referred to as "Highness" and "Majesty". I contrasted this with my matching lowness and whatever holds majesty up, and laughed at the ridiculousness of such titles, but these conventions have consequences that affect us all.

Vaclav Havel said,

> "If every day a man takes orders in silence from an incompetent superior, if every day he solemnly performs ritual acts which he privately finds ridiculous, if he unhesitatingly gives answers to questionnaires which are contrary to his real opinions and is prepared to deny his own self in public, if he sees no difficulty in feigning sympathy or even affection where, in fact, he feels only indifference or aversion, it still does not mean that he has entirely lost the use of one of the basic human senses, namely, the sense of humiliation."

Sounds familiar doesn't it?

A client told me he had "died" while being seriously assaulted. The gang was getting off on his struggles and pleas. He had no options left to survive apart from being dead. The attack had happened some years earlier and yet he was still dead, as was his world.

I said the perpetrators might be coming back anytime and so he was not taking any chances by being alive again.

He said that whoever was coming for him didn't even have to be the original people. He was hyper-vigilant, not-really-dead, not-really-alive, one of the undead, so focused on this event it informed his whole being.

Being alive was the greatest risk of all for him, and yet he was still human in that he knew he was avoiding being alive. Going through the motions is a very human activity, we all do it. His death was a surrender and we worked to make it an honourable act while acknowledging the defeat and humiliation.

Another example of this was given to me by client who said she wished her boyfriend would understand going through the motions. She said he could not keep a job for more than a few months because he just refused to appreciate that this is part of everyday living.

Of course this has two aspects. The downside is what Havel indicates, that a person can be ground down by the horrible meaningless structures of society and those that manage us, compromising integrity bit by bit by bit. The upside is in the enjoyment of the ordinary, a rather alien idea in this culture of chosen ones.

Chosen ones are treated in special ways. It is like being anointed by God. These days, for example, boredom is forbidden for both real and adult children. Some people even go on retreats to be able to sample boredom's gifts.

And yet, we allow ourselves to be entertained into an impersonal trance in front of the TV and computer games. We have become voyeurs living our lives vicariously through footballers and soap stars; the whole celebrity game to which so many of us aspire.

The violence we do to each other and ourselves is in our world; is our world. This violence is based in our fear that life and death are meaningless. To live or die in meaninglessness forever is unbearable. We try to hide from that nightmare by distraction, putting it outside of ourselves as if the outer world were a toxic rubbish dump, a lavatory, forgetting we have to live in it.

Freedom from this is not the opposite of the slavery of the usual we bear every day. It is not isolation, personal, social or cultural. It is not within the person, but in the world that the person is in, which is our world. Freedom is a miracle. Freedom is not a reaction or a choice. Freedom is not born in violent revolution. Violence leads to more violence. Freedom is impossible to attain for it is not a thing to be obtained. The lack of freedom is discovered by noticing the obvious. This is my freedom, my true choice, the noticing of the obvious.

I have as much chance of being free, self actualised and really alive in the sense of not avoiding life, as I have of winning any kind of medal at the next Olympics. There is a very small chance that if no-one else turned up and I walked the 100 metres I would win my medal, and to some that is an attractive proposition.

So what is this freedom anyway? Is freedom that is imposed, even with good intentions, really freedom? Compulsory freedom imposed by force, for your own good, implies that someone knows what is good for you, better than you do. This kind of freedom seems to be predicated on allowing us the freedom to strive for and sometimes attain what we desire.

In this model, even if we are not compelled, freedom cannot be created by being altruistic because the power holders assume selfish desire is the driving force in a free marketplace.

Yet to reach for the stars, to spit in the wind, to stand up and be counted, to do our best rather than try to make up for not being good enough is what makes us miraculous. So of what use is therapy?

Both therapist and client are human. It is another act of violence for the therapist to pretend to be objective, as if I can stand outside the human paradigm that I exist in, that we all create together, able to choose when to relate, and when to be untouched by the other or by my own past, present and future. Withdrawal only exists in relation to contact.

I can never extricate myself from being human. Whatever I am, whatever I feel, whatever I think, whatever I say, everything is of this human paradigm. This includes my grandest visions and the delusion that therapists communicate to clients without the intention of creating an effect, cleaned of suggestion, unpolluted by any agenda.

Our fear of each other, of being here, of not being here,

and the denial of it, breeds a pain that cannot be changed by thinking about it. All of this is compounded and driven by the simple fact that we really do not know what this world is, why this is, where this is, what this is all for, or even if these are valid questions.

The question is, can I take this risk? To share, implicitly and/or explicitly, that I too feel this absence, this separation from a world that I can describe but I really don't know.

Chapter Six • I Want My Medal

Looking into the sky
is looking into infinity
Listening to the silence
is listening to the oldest sound in the universe.
Therapy is an art of the imagination.
Imagining spins the webs of reality.

My intention is to imagine with my client in such a way that imagination being something to avoid, something to fight with, in the guise of those myriad voices of criticism that we all hear, as well as the fascinating horror movies we are glued to, is transformed into a kind of creative imagining. We are experts at this anyway, except we keep creating repetitions, copies of interpretations. Copies of copies of copies.

This process takes a lot of energy to maintain. If energy is going to be spent, I want to spend it with wisdom and timing. Creating the new and honouring the old, this is the natural flow of being and changing to doing and saving, back and forth. You have to be able to do both.

Usual me creates a split in which it is possible for me to experience myself, but I cannot experience myself in the moment, in the here and now. It's the past, the past, the past. Experience is all the various qualities I add to me and you and the world. This is usually based on whether the world is supporting my belief of me in a way that I find acceptable.

I experience you, but what am I experiencing? In the 1970s when I thought I was a bit of a hippy, I had a lot of hair. I grew a really big, black bushy beard. I had this beard for several years. Some friends knew me pre-beard and some friends only knew me with-beard.

One day, on a whim, I shaved it off. I went home and my little daughter, Heidi, who only knew me with-beard, opened the front door to me. She took one look and ran away screaming. She noticed.

There were many people who did not notice. Some did not notice at all. Some asked me if I had lost weight or if I was wearing a new shirt or something. These people knew something was different but were unsure what. A very small percentage of people noticed. I began to think about this. What were the ones who did not notice seeing? Not me. They must be seeing some version of me, a facsimile of me. I think we all do this.

As I experience you, I make my copy of you. The problem is when I interact with my copy of you rather than you, and visa versa. We then have the absurd, tragic and funny situation in which two people are not relating to each other but only to their versions. Of course, there can be certain advantages in this, if you can call it that.

My version of you is so much more controllable and predictable than you. I can know its thoughts and feelings. I can predict its reactions. I can make up whole scenarios and act on them, all without having to contact you or myself. I can place anything about me that I feel unable to contain, both my horrors and my magnificences, in these reproductions, and in this sense these reproductions are a mirror of usual me.

Joan Riviere, taken from an essay by Robert M Young,

"I wish especially to point out... that from the very beginning of life, on Freud's own hypothesis, the psyche responds to the reality of its experiences by interpreting them — or rather, misinterpreting them — in a subjective manner that increases its pleasure and preserves it from pain. This act of subjective interpretation of experience, which it carries out by means of the processes of introjection and projection, is called by Freud hallucination; and it forms the foundation of what we mean by phantasy-life. The phantasy-life of the individual is thus the form in which his real internal and external sensations and perceptions are interpreted and represented to himself in his mind under the influence of the pleasure-pain principle. (It seems to me that one has only to consider for a moment to see that, in spite of all the advances man has made in adaptation of a kind to external reality, this primitive and elementary function of his psyche — to misinterpret his perceptions for his own satisfaction — still retains the upper hands in the minds of the great majority of even civilized adults.)"

I use this notion when I ask my clients what the payoff is for them, what they actually get out of some behaviour or way of thinking. Often they cannot think of any advantage because they assume that it must be a positive payoff, when what they appear to be getting are negative consequences. Quite simply the payoff is what happens.

Sometimes the payoff is in the staging of a fantasy life; a way for usual me to allow itself to be what it believes itself to be. The tamed veneer is stripped away and usual me reveals itself.

Suspension of belief in a book, a film, a computer game, and sexual fantasies, are all releases for this need. Secret behaviours such as bingeing also fulfil usual me's need for symbolic staging of the shadow. We all have a secret life, things that usual me thinks and feels and does when usual me is alone.

Joan Riviere made it quite clear that the payoff is an attraction to the possibility of increased pleasure and the avoidance of pain. That this strategy is often self defeating is all too obvious. For example a person who controls others by losing to them in order to feel secretly superior, or a people pleaser who controls other for personal safety and pleasure.

If I want to please you I must find out what pleases you and find a way to give it to you. In this way I am trying to control your experience of me as a person who, for example, you need. I can then bask in the fake satisfaction of feeling needed by another, maybe even indispensable.

Another aspect of this is in assuming that you need what I need. I think of a client for whom space is a central issue. She is hungry for space and is uncomfortable when others are able to invade her space without her consent.

When she makes an offer to another she always provides a loophole for them to say "no". She gets anxious when others do not provide her with an escape route.

She assumes that others need an escape route, like her, but her provision of this is actually a power situation in that she assumes that they are not equipped with a method of escape if they need it. That escape is her gift to them. This also means she cannot allow another to give her an escape route or try to escape in case they notice.

This was probably born in her power struggle with her parents where saying no was not an option, and there was no escape route from her long term obligations to them.

Another client was struggling with her need to apologise. She had done something, then apologised, then regretted apologising. She had not really apologised anyway; her apology was that she was sorry that the person was hurt. She had not apologised for her actions. I said,

"That gives me the opportunity to say something to you I have really been wanting to say. A few weeks ago you said something that really offended me. I feel so wounded it would be too painful for me to tell you what it was you said. If you say you are sorry it may help to heal my wounds."

For a few moments she thought I was being serious, then the "aha" moment. She disidentified with her usual me, and saw her pattern, her act. She told me she had really wanted to apologise to me, and that until she realised she had fallen into the trap she finds so fascinating, she would have done.

We both laughed. She said she realised that her compulsion to say sorry had nothing to do with me; it was her fantasy based on past incidents in her family. Her insight shone light where darkness has previously reigned. The question is was her new perception any more "real"?

Are we ever in touch with reality? Everything usual me experiences is misinterpretation. My experience of the world is my interpretation of it. In the east this is called maya or illusion. There is individual maya, and also the maya of family, culture and society.

Carlos Castaneda called this the tonal, the personal tonal and the tonal of the times. The tonal of the times is the social usual me that we all share. Understanding this helps me to not take things so personally.

I remember I wanted to catch a bus. I waited in line and when it was my turn to pay, I gave the driver a twenty pound note. I did not have anything smaller. He looked at the note and exploded into a tirade against all the people who had ever given him twenty pound notes. He was red in the face, his eyes were wild, the veins in his neck bulged. I looked around, the bus was full and all the passengers were staring. I looked back at the driver. Eventually he gave me a ticket and my change.

I was full of sympathy for his plight but also glad not to be him. I was expanded and contracted at the same time. This is a useful way of being for a therapist; contracted into the stuff of everyday life, expanded as witness to, the source of, usual me.

My interpretation of the world is the filtering of the information that I perceive, and is performed to suit my own beliefs about me and my world. Usual me gathers evidence that supports usual me's fantasy of who usual me believes myself to be, and tunes everything else out. Proof becomes irrelevant.

Other versions may as well not exist. This is not just an attraction to pleasure and a flight from pain. I may know intellectually that the world is an illusion because it is my interpretation but, for all intents and purposes, this usual me world of Geoffrey is real because it is the only real that is available to him. Geoffrey cannot leave Geoffrey land.

Riviere talks about "real internal and external sensations and perceptions". Real in what sense? She is assuming a real world that is knowable, but who is it that knows? Who is the difference between internal and external, the space between this and that. It sounds like the Abbott and Costello story, "Who's on first base?"

Is she referring to the true me world, where contradiction is unity or the usual me world where contradiction is division, the roots of comparison and prejudice? Thinking is discrimination. These are not two discreet worlds that come and go, but always here, implicit in each other. I am in one or the other depending on whether I am usual me or true me.

It is in the usual world that we must learn to meet with each other. It is in the usual me world we must practice the language of intimacy by honouring maya, the "ten thousand things" as Lao Tsu named the spectrum of the usual me world. Honouring is not pandering.

Speaking this language, cherishing the usual me, we can make the kind of contact that allows both of us to know what it is to be with an other, not to feel so alone and frightened, and yet not to deny our loneliness and fear. In some small way we are then redressing the alienation that occurred when contact was violent by its absence as well as by its presence.

This is the practice of being, being aware of my body as my environment, but not me as a subject and my body as object. This includes sensations, emotions and thoughts. Geoffrey is the sensations, the emotions, and the thoughts, all physical processes. Geoffrey is a body experience, no body, no Geoffrey. But this is not just an inner process. I exist in a living world.

Can usual me be mindful of its relationship with the world and style of relating? Can usual me be aware of usual me's judgements, usual me's bestowal of qualities? Can usual me be aware that you think and feel? Can usual me be aware of usual me filtering? Can usual me hear and understand the symbolic clues about the here and now world that expanded true me gives usual me?

Recently I had to have some medical treatment. I have had problems with my spine since I was 17 and involved in a car crash in Spain. My doctor sent me for an MRI scan. I was put in a machine that magnetised my molecules for half an hour while they photographed my spine.

What was interesting for me was my paranoia. It was almost instantaneous. Previously I had only noticed paranoid self-talk and pictures, but in the confines of the machine I became aware of the physical nature of it. It swept up in waves from my feet. It was a very primitive feeling akin to the way I experienced grief when my father died.

As the paranoia swept up my body and reached my torso, my breathing changed and became panting, high in my chest. I got hot and as it reached my head the paranoid stories and pictures began. I was able to cope by breathing down into my diaphragm. I was calm for a while then the process repeated. It was a physical experience and I learned, once again, the physical nature of thoughts and images, rather than them being something abstract.

The world will also mirror my paranoia. Last week I had a gastroscopy for the first time. I went into the hospital, got a needle stuck in the back of my hand ready for the sedation, and then sat in the waiting area. I began to imagine all the things that could go wrong; the tube damaging something in me, gagging and having to pull the tube out of my throat etc. etc.

The next two patients arrived and began to discuss the procedure which they had both had before. They were saying my thoughts out loud. One said, "I hate this, the last time I was here the sedation didn't work, I began to gag and pulled the tube out of my throat myself." The other one said, "I hate the spray they use to freeze your throat. It tastes terrible and made my gagging reflex worse."

I looked at them as they continued, judged them to be very different from me, and yet we were connected by our humanity, the social usual me. Usual me began to laugh at itself. My paranoia was gone. It was no longer mine. I was no longer taking it personally. Usual me calmed down.

◆

Chapter Seven • Making Movies

A life of regret
is no life at all
And what's life if you pull punches?
Safely asleep,
dreaming of love
And what's love if you're unconscious?

A young woman walks heavily into my room. I can feel gravity increasing. I feel weighed down. She looks distressed. Her eyes are a little red and dart about as she talks. Immediately, I am listening, looking, feeling, wondering, and waiting to be invited into a sort of contact that does not attempt to demystify or solve confusion, but does involve the use of manipulation.

All forms of communication can be described as manipulative. I want to influence you. I want to create an effect. I notice how people describe the world to themselves; the words, the tone, the tempo, the movement and quality of the dance between us. This includes analysing and witnessing, and by using process comments and sharing my judgements, I hope to create a beneficial effect.

Clients say, "I want you to understand me in the way I want to be understood, for you to see through my games and bullshit in the way I want you to see through them." If you engage me as your therapist, you are expecting something. I too am expecting something. We both have our agendas. We are both in a trance.

She begins to talk. She tells me, with anguish in her voice and fear and pain in her eyes, that she is crying, she can't sleep properly, she is making mistakes at work. She says she is confused, doesn't know who she is anymore, she does things and thinks things that are not like her. She has become a stranger to herself. She can never love again. And how did all this happen? Her boyfriend deceived her by having an affair with one of her friends.

At first, he denied it and said she was crazy. He assured her of his love and his loyalty. He denied her experience and she let him. She wanted her intuition to be wrong because she wanted him. Her usual me had been wounded.

Now she feels fooled. She is angry with herself for letting him trick her. "What a fool I am" she says to herself. But she won't let go. She talks to herself about it, over and over. She tortures herself with pictures of them enjoying themselves, on holiday, having great sex, being intimate with each other.

As she shares this with me she has a sort of triumphal smile on her face, even a sparkle in her eye. I know some part of her is actually enjoying it.

She won't let go and move on with her life, her usual me will not allow it. Her usual me is trying instead to withdraw, to deaden her environment. She is draining colour from her world and feeling justified. This was her usual me attempting to acclimatise to the situation.

She says she wants him to say he is sorry, that he was wrong, and that he loves her really. Not only will she not let go of the past but, more importantly, her fantasy; the fantasy of a perfect future together in quite an advanced stage of guarantee.

Who can let go of the possibility of perfection? The fantasy of her ex and his new lover being intimate friends and lovers is painfully magnetic. What is the difference between attraction and repulsion?

And why will usual me not let go? Because if she lets go then she suspects she will be ok, and if she is ok now that denies how not ok the past was, that it wasn't that bad. If she is ok now that denies the reality of her pain and she is not about to have her reality denied again, especially by herself. Usual me has become an accomplice to the crime and continues to torture her as he tortured her.

Usual me sees this as survival oriented behaviour. This behaviour becomes a well practised routine in reaction to usual me's not good enough beliefs about itself which it projects onto the world and then experiences as the environment acting on it.

Her wasted life is a monument to the death she cannot accept, a marker of the crime that occurred, an ongoing cry of remembrance to the pain that must never be forgotten, and so lived in the present.

So what does she want from me? Her usual me wants to know that another person acknowledges her pain, that death is real. All her friends are trying to help her by denying her pain. I acknowledge it, unrequited love is painful.

At first she was angry, it was his entire fault. Being the effect of something easily transforms into being a victim. She had got trapped in this particular usual me with its attendant narrative and consequences. When she realised this, together we fantasized a new myth in which it was healthy for her to have acted and felt in the way she did, but enough now. Her future is open again.

She always knew that her part in it had been her part in it, but she had denied it in the face of her pain. Her usual me needed pain to be validated. She needed to find some meaning in her betrayal, and not to have been an accident.

She needed to trust her perception again. At first, it will be a bit scary. She may be rejected again, and this is her challenge, to take that risk, to return to life. As Dave Jones, my supervisor said to me, "Reflection is the antidote to reaction."

A person who comes into therapy asking to be healed of pain is also asking to be healed of love. The moment I say "I love you" I give you the power to hurt me. The moment I give you my trust, the possibility of betrayal is created.

Sooner or later I will be parted from everything and everybody I love. I can live now or I can regret and grieve. Love and suffering are inextricably combined, for the nature of love is that the intensity of its passion is fuelled by the pain of its potential and actual loss. This is the great challenge of relationship, and what makes the journey so worthwhile.

◆

Chapter Eight • Risk

Only the lost seek to be found,
Attaching like limpets to anything
with even a hint of security,
Then complaining about the lack of freedom

Every time a new client arrives in my room, I am entering into a world that is fraught with risk, not just for the client, but for me, and the dangers are many. My friend, Mark Foster, is working in Ireland with survivors of sexual abuse by religious orders. This is a high risk occupation for him.

I also run the same risks but not as concentrated. He is listening to, experiencing and reacting to horrors on a daily basis. Make no mistake, this is not vicarious, the person is in the room with him. Usual me has a shadow and it is this that gets interested, gets excited. Prurience is real, it is a physical experience. My way of describing it is that my dark side is like fronds or ferns that wave about. When they sense the dark side in another they get excited and want to make contact, to engage.

I recognise the compulsive aspects of this. When I am with someone describing something dark, I can feel that part of usual me getting curious, wanting to ask questions and make remarks that will steer the conversation ever darker.

This is how transference works, parts recognising counterparts and attempting to connect with each other and to communicate with each other. It is like accepting an invitation to dance.

Mark told me he went to a seminar on this subject and one of the exercises was to imagine going up to a school playground, looking through the railings and picking which child you might fancy. There was uproar in the room and some people walked out. Even the fantasy was a sin. And yet if I am to work with the darkness, I must find some way of dealing with it in the therapy and personally for myself. If a human being does something, I too have the potential to do it. Legislating against the dark side does not make it go away.

I risk being wounded. This can happen in one take if the client finds a button of mine that I am unaware of, or it can be a drip that grinds into my consciousness until we are reverberating together but at a different rhythm to a different tune. This is confusing at best and potentially very bad for my health.

Some therapists use rituals to cleanse themselves of their client's energy but prevention is best. This is not achieved by resistance. Can I include my own vulnerability and yet be strong? Can I be conscious of the temporary nature of my life and my client's life and put this in some context for myself?

We are all on a planet that spins and hurtles through space at thousands of miles a minute. The Earth, our solar system, the Milky Way; we are never in the same place twice.

Wherever this is, wherever we have been, and wherever we are headed, this familiar hall of mirrors that usual me surrounds itself with for security reasons, is only familiar because of my incessant talking about it to myself.

I can point to lots of things and say their names, but I have no idea what this is. I find believing this very freeing. It helps me to lighten up, not to take things so personally, not to buy just because someone is selling, even me. I can only hang onto something if I believe myself to be somebody. The thing is, who?

Another risk is if I can allow myself to be the baddy. Now I know I like to be liked. I definitely prefer my client to experience me as warm, caring and empathic. Yet sometimes that will not do therapeutically. It may be very nice socially but it is just plain bullshit in therapy. I know this and yet the risk is there, plus the modern risk of litigation. How many conversations do therapists have privately about covering their backs?

The client may have had a cold disapproving father. I can easily be the warm approving father and sometimes that is the thing, but at some point the real clincher is to be able to be the cold disapproving one. Now I know I said "be" but its more like taking the mantle of, acknowledging the cold disapproving part of me and my judgements of that part. I do not want to be all that, and there is the risk, actually identifying with that me too closely, confluence with a fragment.

One of the effects is that the client might not like me for introducing something like this. It may be wrong in some way. It may be experienced as not mine to introduce, bad timing, or an act of betrayal of the confidence they have placed in me.

Unless something new is introduced into therapy, how can change occur? Not with the same old stuff. Necessarily this must come from outside of the client's frame of reference.

In the transference, the client will inevitably press my buttons, as I will press their buttons. Counter transference is a misnomer; it assumes a leader and a follower. Transference is mutually arising. Part of the other's usual me and part of my usual me meet and interact. In my experience the more psychotic the client, the more likely they are to hone in exactly to the part I would rather not know about.

In the early 1990s, I was working in an old Victorian psychiatric hospital in London. I was a part time bank nurse, which meant I was put onto any ward that was short of staff. At first I worked on the geriatric wards, which was mostly about the conveyor belt of feeding, toileting and medicating.

After a few months I was assigned to an acute admission ward, which housed severely disturbed people. We had an enlightened Irish ward manager called John Bunyan. I remember him saying to me "If you can't be mad in a psychiatric hospital, where can you?"

This is the meaning of asylum, a safe place for breakdown and breakthrough. I liked the old Victorian psychiatric hospitals. Mad people need both containing and the space to be as mad as they can be.

One morning, I arrived for the start of my shift and walked around the ward to see what was going on, ready and eager to "help" someone.

I went into the dining room. It was a very large room, with several huge picture windows. The ward was on the second floor and as the hospital stood in its own grounds, almost a park, there was a lovely view. The floor in the dining room was covered with shiny flecked lino. The sun shone in through the windows and I could see the dust sparkling in the air.

There were tables and chairs in a sort of horseshoe arrangement. In the centre of the room sat a new patient, a woman, all alone, head in hands, slumped onto the table. She seemed dwarfed by the room, and I felt a pang in my heart. I imagined how alone I would feel in her place. I contrasted the sunshine and her seemingly dark mood. So, full of it, I walked over to her. She did not acknowledge my presence.

I said, "Hello, I'm Geoffrey, how are you today?" She turned and looked at me straight in the eyes. "You're a nosey little Jew boy cunt!" she said smiling. The force of her words actually knocked me back, I nearly fell over. I experienced the part of me that was exactly that. It was my shame at that part of me that was so shocking. I was so modern now; I had done so much work on myself.

To discover in one go that I was still a nosey little Jew boy and recognised as one, was unbearable. It was not who I wanted to be, it was definitely not how I wanted others to view me. I forgot that "nosey little Jew boy" are just words. I hardly noticed the word "cunt".

Usual me thought it was so smart and had all the angles covered. This came from a direction that usual me in its bloated self importance had completely discounted.

I learned a lot in that hospital. Every time I pushed the heavy ward door open I stepped through the looking glass into an alternate reality with its own strange rules, but every "door" I walk through is the same.

The ward where I worked was massive, with high ceilings and large rooms. Everywhere needed painting and refreshing, especially the bathroom with its peeling magnolia paint, cracked tiles and rusting pipes.

I was going to say that the bathroom smelled, but the whole place smelled, not like the geriatric wards where the air was heavy with old urine molecules, but similar in feel, hopeless and resigned, where passion meant madness and was frowned on by the staff. Passionate patients were too much work, much better if they were docile and did what they were told.

It wasn't that the patients were mistreated as such, but that they had to stick to rules whose purpose was to make them malleable and docile because this was a large part of how "getting better" was defined.

There was a blackmail element to some of the patients being there, a sort of double bind. To compel a patient to take the prescribed medication, the patient had to be on a treatment section. Some of the patients were voluntary and would not take the medication.

The blackmail was that they were told that if they did not take the medication they would be sectioned. They took the medication. This got around the chore of having to get someone sectioned with all the attendant paperwork. It was too time consuming for everyone, easier to get "consent". Many of the rights that we take for granted did not apply to a sectioned patient. If someone is in prison at least they know the length of their sentence.

I made friends with some of the patients. I remember a young slight woman who would stand for hours gazing out of the picture windows. I had learned by now to approach people more quietly. So I stood next to her for quite some time, gazing with her, before I wondered out loud what we were waiting for.

"A space ship to land", she said, still gazing at the sky. That sounded quite attractive, who knows? So I asked her if it was alright for me to wait with her. "If you like" she replied.

So I stood with her and waited. Eventually we began, hesitantly at first, to have little conversations about ordinary things. She was an interesting person. Then one of the senior nurses pulled me to one side, and asked me what we were talking about. I told him about the spaceship. He told me not to do that anymore. He said I would make things worse if I went into her psychotic world, I was validating the psychosis.

There was no point in arguing with him. That was exactly how to get to her, to be accepted by her. We had got to the ordinary through the psychotic. Anyway, I figured it was symbolic of something, but I never did find out what. After this when that nurse was on shift, I did not stand with her so often but I still entered into her reality if invited. It was the human thing to do.

I was attacked once. I was on a break, sitting reading

the newspaper in the hall-like corridor outside the nurse's office. The office had a door with a window. The window was made out of a thick sheet of plastic. It was so scratched it was hard to see detail through it. I heard a loud bang.

I looked up just in time to see a very large new male patient headed for me very fast. He had just come right through the door, which was now hanging off its hinges, and he was charging right at me. He shouted "I'll kill you!" Instinctively, I stood up and we slammed into each other and fell over.

In an instant all the other nurses were there pulling him off me. They sat on him, and held him down. They were well prepared for this sort of thing. In moments a nurse appeared with a hypodermic and he was injected in his buttock. Gradually he stopped struggling and they carried him into the bedroom and lay him on his bed.

I was given a cup of hot sweet tea. I was still shaking. I sat in the nurses' tea room turning the event over in my mind. What was so chilling was that it had not been personal. He was a new patient. We had never talked. I just happened to be in his sights. He would have tried to kill me without even knowing my name, let alone who I was. Is that better or worse than being killed by someone who knows me?

We lived in California in the 1980s, spending time with friends who were into consciousness and new paradigms. When I first met the gestalt teachers at Esalen Institute, I could not understand them at all. They scared the shit out of me. I thought they could read my mind. After hanging out with them I got that they were living gestalt, not just theoretically as a technique in the groups they led, but in their everyday lives.

What really got me was that they were themselves, idiosyncratic, willing to live out their imperfections. I wanted them to be perfect, nice, caring all the time. I wanted them to like me so I tried to live up to my idea of who I thought they thought

I should be around them, my idealised version of them. I soon got this was not a good idea as they called me on it and made fun of me every chance I gave them. How I struggled and suffered before I surrendered and got it.

In one of our early English groups we used to present an exercise called high horse. We would ask people to dress up and get on their high horse and gallop around the room repeating their high horse phrase to the other participants. My phrase was, "Out of my way, don't you know who I am?" The following is an example of my usual me's high horsiness.

When we returned to England in the late 1980s my wife got a job teaching ceramics at a college in Essex. One day we were in Romford for the first time, and I fancied a Kentucky Fried Chicken. We were still eating meat in those days. There was a queue of about a dozen people.

As we were waiting two young women came in. They were loud and a bit drunk. They walked to the front of the line and demanded to be served. The people at the front agreed. I said, "Hold on I don't agree to this." They walked over to me, right in my face and began swearing and verbally abusing me.

Full of California and of being in groups where honesty was not just recommended but demanded, only recently back in England, not realising what these girls were like, and full of usual me self importance, I said, "You must have a lot of pain in your heart to act like this, go home and talk it through with your mother."

I assume I was spot on because her immediate reaction was to punch me on the jaw, knock me to the ground and share her pain with me. We wrangled around for some time while the spectators merely spectated. Nobody, including my wife did anything. She said she felt frozen. It was one of those slow motion events. Eventually the police arrived and settled things down.

The next week Carole joined a karate club, eventually becoming a third dan black belt. She said she was never going to be a bystander like that again. Years later she told me that one of the things she learned from karate was how to stay conscious when hitting or being hit.

The shadow side of this is someone who gets hit or hits until they turn off consciousness in order to survive, like my client who "died". I suppose it depends on the context.

This is also an example of one of usual me's survival strategies, the ability to dissociate from a painful event. In this case Carole called it "freezing". Another way to describe it is "leaving your body". Many people are uncomfortable in their bodies and are "out of it" as we used to say.

A client who was a prostitute would put her consciousness into a light bulb on the ceiling that she had to have switched on while she was having sex with her clients. It was how she coped when she was abused as a child. This worked ok until one of her clients insisted on turning the light off. She freaked out as she had nowhere to go.

The NLP approach uses dissociation in its phobia techniques. For some chronic pain sufferers dissociating from their pain is the best and only option. It is like dreaming or day dreaming in which I either see myself in the action or I am in the action.

Freeze framing is a defensive strategy. It contains the hope that at some later date, the situation that could not be born at that time can be unfrozen, reintroduced into the world and completed. The problem is when I get trapped in the escape.

I remember working with a teenager who had taken a lot of LSD in one go, and was experiencing flashbacks of the time just previous to his ingesting the drug. This was occurring at about one minute intervals.

His body was jerking in time to the flashbacks. He was in

hospital on sedation, but it was not working. What did work was to take him back purposely to the original event and encourage him to re-experience it. In this way he was able to move from victim position to source position. The more he went through it on purpose, the slower the flashback cycle became. This took a few hours.

He needed to regress in order to heal, but in a safe and containing environment. He remade his relationship with the usual me that had taken the drug. He was no longer the victim of himself.

Our ability to do this is a parallel of how we do not need to identify with usual me, but can step backstage, so to speak, and identify with, be, true mind, the source of usual me.

I remember attending a lecture by the Dalai Lama, when he was suggesting something similar. His language was that it was possible to meditate on a particular divine being, to be it from the inside and to practice the attributes associated with it.

The very act of recognising parts is divisive. It separates I into lots of usual mes, like a prism splitting light. I am also separating from the world, everything "outside" me. Usual mes define themselves in this way and it is the nature of usual me to desire, especially to be special.

Special can mean lots of different things. It can mean not being an accident or fixed by fate or genes. But prisms work both ways and we can start with where we are, at usual me, or we can be at the other shore, not knowing what the journey will bring.

Do I go for work with parts, the usual mes? Do I follow the separate to integrate rule? Do I experiment with identifying with expanded true me as a model? Do I go for manipulating my client into realising that he is who he is, exactly as he is, all of him? And that if he is going to wait until he is loveable until he loves himself, he will wait a long time?

But parts are a handy way of talking about something,

the human being, which is not easy to describe because I am a human being. Again it comes to trusting the process, the Holy of Holies of therapy. At Esalen, I was always told, "Don't interfere with the process."

There is a religious aspect to the therapy movement, no matter how much the researchers and the psychologists play the game of being scientists, but human relationship cannot be reduced to faith or fact, neither tells the whole story.

Kabir, the controversial mystic, who constantly proclaimed his mad love for God,

> "There is nothing but water at the holy bathing places; and I know that they are useless because I have bathed in them.
> The images are all lifeless, they cannot speak; I know for I have cried aloud to them.
> The Purana and the Koran are mere words; lifting up the curtain I have seen.
> Kabir gives utterance to the words of experience; and he knows very well that all other things are untrue."

Psychotherapy and psychology have their holy bathing places, holy images, holy books, prophets, heretics and apostates.

Chapter Nine • Sex

In a trance, logic gone,
But still there are fantasies and the dreamer.
I lose my mind,
Wanting, wanting to be wanted,
I am a crazy man.

Usually when I read about sex and therapy, it is hidden under the banner of the erotic. The fact is there is also sex, and whenever people are together there is always the potential for sex to occur.

The very boundaries and confidentiality we all hold so dear, that create a safe space for a person to express themselves and share their secrets with another is a contributing factor to this possibility. The regular appointments, the closed door, the limited time, the intimacy, the secrets shared, are all components of a romantic rendezvous.

I remember working with a prostitute who remarked how similar therapy was to her work, and how strange she felt being in client position paying a fee to me.

Human beings are inordinately interested in sex. We are fascinated with it in all its variations. To admit publicly that I too am fascinated promotes excitement and fear in me.

Why should this be? Why do therapists rarely own that we are sexual beings, not separate from the rest of the herd in this either. For safety I assume, but we are embodied beings, lustful, interested in our bodies and other bodies too.

I am not suggesting that it is ok for therapists to have sex with their clients. Sex with a client constitutes an abuse of power, but that is part of the attraction for both people. It is a mistake to pretend that sex is nice and clean and clinical. Sex is not logical; it makes no sense, and is never equal.

Sex is not just physical. When experienced as a repetitive set of movements, it can become absurd. Fantasy is what makes it exciting, and imbalance is part of the fantasy. What constitutes abuse in one context can be experienced as the heights of ecstasy in another situation. A sexual equal opportunity policy would be ridiculous and unworkable.

I often hear therapists talk about leaving their "stuff" by the door as they enter the therapy room. Even if this were possible, as my daughter remarked, "Why pick it up again?" So why imagine that it is possible, even desirable, to leave sexual feelings and fantasy "by the door"? Our stock in trade is fantasy and imagination, and the therapist must be brave enough to acknowledge usual me's sexual fantasies as an essential part of the therapeutic relationship.

That sex between therapist and client is such a taboo suggests the amount of fascination it holds, as all taboos do. If a magnetic pull is to be resisted, it has to be countered relative to its power.

Shame is another reason to avoid this subject. I remember being on a two year course. We were in the second year and the students had got to know each other quite well. We were having a theoretical discussion about attraction to clients, and the other man in our group of about twenty said that he if he got an erection in a session he excused himself and went out for a while until his erection had subsided. Whether this was the right course of action is open to discussion, but it was the negative reaction from most females in the group which was interesting.

The man was basically shamed for having an erection at all. The general consensus was that he should have controlled himself. I was so shocked that, regretfully, I said nothing for fear of being shamed too. However, body excitement, not just the nicer abstract kind, could occur for both male and female therapists. How many dare to take this to supervision and utilise it therapeutically?

So what to do with all this? What should I do if I fancy a client, if I get excited? Well, what do we do with any of what occurs in the therapy relationship? Is this any different?

The stories we tell each other are based on memories and fantasies stored in and around the body, interpretations of the past. They are of the same substance as dreams, and in the therapeutic situation can be explored in the same way.

Sexual attraction stories are no different. Whether our feelings are real or not is not the issue. If usual me is bored or excited or whatever while being with my client, that is grist for the therapeutic mill as Ram Dass put it.

The erotic, in this case the sex slipstream of it, is about the attraction of mystery, the excitement of knowing and not knowing what is happening. There is a trance like quality to this energy, it ignores the rules by not being aware of them, or makes them a reason to continue. It can be experienced with another, but in this slipstream sometimes usual me cannot be swayed by the consequences on others, and sometimes it is because of the consequences.

Therapists, by the nature of the relationship, are in a different role to their clients. Clients go to therapists and not the other way round. We both have an agenda.

I want my client to realise they have choices in their

lives, no matter how seemingly unpalatable they are. I want them to know that another person knows them as a person, and communicates that, not just in what they say, or by some technique, but because it is true. I also want to be perceived in a certain way. I want to have a particular effect on another.

I was working with a woman who apparently did not like me. I'll call her Mary. She was aggressive and petulant. She alternated between long silences in which she swung her legs over the arm of her chair and stared into space, and turning her head, glaring at me and then looking away again.

I did my process comments, and gradually fell into trying to resist my judgments. Any comment I made she turned back on me, telling me that was only my opinion, or dismissing my remark with a deep sigh. I began to dread her arrival and breathe a sigh of relief at her departure.

She was in her thirties but I experienced her like the stroppiest of teenagers. I shared this with her, I asked her what it did for her, but again she rejected me. I told her I felt rejected and attacked, she laughed in my face. "What kind of therapist are you? Call yourself a counsellor?" she sneered, "Didn't you do any training?" I told her I felt defensive, and she said that wasn't right, that a proper counsellor wouldn't be defensive and that I was making it all about me, another sin of course.

Sometimes she would sob quietly, her face turned away from me. She never told me why. Part of me felt sorry for the pain she was in, but I was frustrated, hurt and angry. I was as rejecting with myself as she was with me. She did not want my empathy.

I concluded that any attempt at showing her I cared highlighted her inability to be intimate with another. I became progressively disabled. Rather than trusting the process, I tried to force it as a means of denying my own shame of not being good enough and my desire to abandon her. I did this by becoming petulant and aggressive myself.

The counselling finished on a sour note. She accused me of finishing prematurely. We had agreed a fixed number of sessions, and she said she has two more. I checked the dates, but she would not have it, and although I had never been good enough, she wanted more. I said this to her. She said I was just like everyone else. She said "I'm glad I never trusted you. I knew you would let me down."

The erotic connection had been made and was being expressed in terms of her experience of my premature withdrawal and her rage with me for frustrating her need to achieve a satisfying orgasm. This said something of both our needs to punish and be punished. We had assumed positions from the past. She was whoever had hurt her, employing the same methods, and I was her, partly energised and informed by my past, hurt and not allowed to defend myself.

It also reflected my need to get the whole damn thing over with as well as not wanting to be in touch with the fact that she was right about me not wanting to be with her anymore. I felt I had let both of us down. The best I could manage was to remind myself "This too shall pass."

I also noticed that as this process was unfolding the "bad" me was ever more focussed on this particular interaction, and the "nice" me became even "nicer" to my other clients. This was expressed by me being much less challenging with them.

A few weeks after we parted, I received a three page letter. It was a long harangue abusing me about my shortcomings as a person and as a counsellor. As I read it, my heart sank. Was she going to complain about me? Was I that bad? What was it I had not addressed? Were there some associations I had missed?

I had taken her to supervision several times. Eventually, after nights of interrupted sleep, I was able to put the letter aside. I rationalised it by saying it was just a client sounding off as some do, and that at least we had made some contact.

Five years later, I received a card. On the front was a beautiful print of Tibetan prayer flags flying on a mountainside. It was from Mary.

She said she was sending me a belated apology and that she was sorry for any pain or hurt she had caused me. She thanked me for the help I had given her. She said how much she had appreciated me being caring and accepting, and how I had been a safety net for her. Now she was a Buddhist, a practising meditator and was experiencing positive movement in her life. She ended by wishing me well.

It is quite a while since I thought about this incident and quite a while since I read the letters. Unfortunately, not her first one, I threw it away as I tried to move on from my hurt feelings, hoping to throw the experience away.

I told myself that the incident was complete and therefore over, but it was not. I did not express this in my reply. I shared my realisation that I had been a safe target for her, but I did not tell her that it had not been safe for me.

I was still protecting myself, and yet I was still trying to communicate that I cared for her and accepted her. I think what this means for me is being intimate with the other person by being myself, as I am.

While I was being myself, she was being herself and we both stuck at it. We were together, for example, in the conflict of my wish to stop seeing her, for me to avoid my anxiety of realising my regrets too late as I die, and her wish to avoid, yet to be fascinated with, the failure of her life in its latest incarnation, the failure of the therapy.

We both suffered, but we made a vital and passionate contact, we were vulnerable to each other, we had spoken to each other in the language of intimacy. We had shared the reality of mutual conflict, an essential part of any relationship.

Chapter Ten • Permission Granted

The ins and outs
The ups and downs
The secrets kept
The going round
And each one plays their lonely game
And every day is just the same.

People come into therapy as perpetrators, victims, survivors, and bystanders, combining them in different ways, and moving from one valence to another. They tell stories and demonstrate their physical, emotional, mental and spiritual attitudes to life.

Sometimes when I read them I manage reasonable guesses at what these might mean. If I decide to tell my client I hope that she will do something with my guess that somehow seems to make a difference. Sometimes I lay out options. Any and all communications are interferences with another or me.

My agenda is for them to experience that they are the source of their particular usual me stuff, mirrored by the usual me stuff of this particular culture in this particular era.

My interference is manipulative. Manipulation has a bad press these days. It is about being skilful. I like that the NLP people describe this as sleight of mouth. It could be expanded to sleight of being, the Mercury/Trickster/Magician archetype. The twenty two cards of the major arcana of the tarot deck provide valuable insights into the kind of archetypes with which therapists can identify.

I can be the Fool, teetering on the edge of the abyss of the unknown, willing to be naïve and ask the obvious to try to understand. I can be the Hierophant/Rabbi, steeped in tradition, dispensing wisdom. I can be the Emperor, imperiously ruling by divine right and edict.

Sometimes people need permission to be, do, or have. They know that ultimately permission is theirs to give, not mine, but they need to hear it from another, a confirmation.

A man in his thirties arrives, average height. He has a strong local accent, and is dressed like a man who works outside with his hands. He appears nervous. He doesn't look at me much, just little, almost furtive, glances as if to check me out, but I am not supposed to notice this, so I don't.

I play people's usual me games for a little while; it is part of the creation of rapport. Later, when I no longer collude, no longer say yes so often, that makes my no much more powerful. Our domain is the imagination, not facts, and in that area I can share my sense of wonder about the world and the struggles and pain of life that none of us avoid.

We give another the power to transport us into heaven and into hell. Where are the facts in that? Every time I can be vulnerable enough to be intimate, I am opening my heart to a myth in which the world is alive and we can dream a loving dream, where the shadow defines the light rather than being a monster that devours me.

This man's monster was his interpretation of his

relationship with his father. His father had been strict and literally commanded his son's respect into being. He was trying the same with his own boys, but they were not responding how there were supposed to, which was how he had always responded.

My client followed orders out of a sense of duty, rather than love. It was like being in the army. He had never felt loved or lovable and that was why respect had become so important, really he was a beggar for love, always in deficit. "DON'T SPEAK. DON'T SHOW FEELING."

We could have practised some form of thought blocking in which negative thoughts are challenged. We could have made a list of positive thoughts to use as tools to do this. But positive and negative thoughts are polar opposites connected to each other by context. Up has no meaning without down. We could have come from people being innately "good" but these approaches are basically avoidance, disrespecting the shadow.

To accept another is also to be aware that I deny him. Can I share both my acceptance and my denial? This is a confirmation of the person in the relationship now, as it is. It is not by force that a person can discard the old and embrace the new.

Anyway, the old is to be respected. It is how I got to be here. I would rather say thank you to my old patterns and put them out to a peaceful retirement in a nice green pasture, than send them to the knacker's yard.

Too often the language of therapy itself is individualistic. We talk from usual me. We approach the therapy as usual me, we contact each other as usual me. This is only half the story. There is an intimate language of us. The context of this language is the world as a place to share, and that we are all in this together.

The micro and the macro co-exist. Could usual me speak such a language? What would happen?

When I realized I was the current substitute for his father, I gave him consent to love his sons and to be kind to them.

That was the therapy. It balanced the severity of his prohibition on loving with a mercy he yearned for, rather than blocking or denying or even confronting it to get to his "real self".

There is no real self. The self makes itself up moment by moment. This means the past is not set, history is different with each creation. This man needed permission from his father to love his own sons. We got to know each other a little and then a simple acknowledgment by both of us of what he needed. Once I had given consent, he knew it was his all along. He was no longer in deficit. He could open his heart a little and dare to love. He had new orders.

Chapter Eleven • Attention

His eyes swept over the dark valley to the ocean beyond. The sky was full of stars and a crescent moon floated in the heavens. "A glowing example of levitation" he said laughing.
And the silence; each sound in that silence was a miracle, an insect moving, the popping of embers in the barbecue pit, a zephyr whispering its way through the dark blue trees.
Breathing in the warm smell of eucalyptus and redwood, he put his hand to his neck to check if he was real. The vein moved rhythmically beneath his fingers. Gradually he quieted down.
Scarcely talking to himself, the parade of mind pictures went into slow motion. He gazed into one that hung before him, expanding and contracting with the beating of his heart. And then in the midst of the darkness, a light, a small light until she was floating in front of him, swaying like a Chinese lantern.
"I'm dreaming you aren't I?" he heard his voice say.
"Yes," she said, "in a way."
She held out her hand to him and he took it and helped her to step down onto the grass.
"Well, she said, "I thought you were never going to wake up!"

It is obvious that the therapist should pay attention, but to what? I am not talking about attending to the complicated stories that people tell, although stories are important ways of passing and filling the time, sometimes permission to be in therapy.

Rehearsed stories are interesting examples of patterns, unrehearsed stories can be cathartic for the client, but I am waiting for the spontaneous, the small and the simple, a moment, a mime, a gesture, a communication that could be missed because of its banality, its ordinariness, its clumsiness, its abstract nature, its grace, or its apparent irrelevance.

I need to be tuned in to noticing things like this, and not to be prescriptive about what arrives. Bill and William is a good example of this.

Bill came to see me over several months. He seemed a thoughtful man, tall and a little slow in his movements. He appeared to be holding back, not just from me but from his life. I was just part of that. He was on a counselling course.

It is always interesting working with students of whatever age. Students who attend counselling, because of a course requirement, can be a challenge. They know some counselling theory and are gaining experience as placement counsellors, unpaid volunteers, yet paying for the course, supervision and therapy.

The whole notion of money and therapy is loaded with stuff. Usually when I give my money to someone, not as a gift but in exchange for something, I get something that I knew I would get from the start. Therapy is not like that. We do not know where we will go together. There is no arrival at a predetermined destination. I am offering some being time together.

Counselling students come expecting to see a real counsellor in action, someone with whom they can be disappointed, admire and envy. They discuss their therapist as much as their therapy with fellow students. They get disappointed if their friend cries all the time in counselling and they have not shed one tear with me.

They are fearful they will inadvertently make some terrible mistake and permanently damage someone. What they are learning is the language of therapy, an academic version at college, and the Geoffrey version during the time we are together. I call this intimate language and speaking it allows us to explore the human condition as it acts through us. Then we can laugh and cry and wonder together at the magnificence and the tragedy of it all. Then somehow we know we are in this together.

Bill was telling me again about his new assertive behaviour. He said his wife had always made decisions for both of them. He had never chosen an article of clothing for himself since they were married.

All the clothes he was wearing were hand-me-downs from his children. As he was telling me all this, I noticed him move his head to the right, away from me I felt, and say something like "My wife said, William...." and then what she said. The word "William" was said more quietly than the rest of the sentence.

He carried on with his story. William? I knew him as Bill. Here was the small thing I had been waiting for. He had made William stand out by a small head movement and the change of volume. I am sure I would have disappointed him if I had not picked up his clue.

When I pointed this out to him, he explained that he had made a conscious decision to become a new person by becoming Bill to all the people he had met since he started his course, including me. Now we were able to open communication between these two parts, to understand the differences and similarities in terms of their wants and needs, fears and hopes, dreams and disappointments.

He could experience William's feelings of inadequacy and worthlessness, what he named "Get-by William", and Bill's fledgling drive and ambition. How easy is it to notice things like this? It is easy if I am patient and attending to the here and now, speaking the language of intimacy. Impossible if I am unaware that I am experiencing you as an object whether partial or whole. I am not even sure there is such a thing as a whole object.

Do we just infer wholes from parts? If usual me is not whole, and it is not because it splits, then how can usual me experience something whole?

Today we were talking about what he wanted when he first came into therapy. He said "I said I didn't do feelings and I wanted to get in touch with them. I thought that meant falling on the floor and crying and then I could put that up on the wall like a poster, that I had done it. Now I know it's nothing to do with that. I know I've got bucketfuls of emotion to give and I have given to certain selected people. But if I want to give that more generally I have to be prepared to take the risk of the occasional rejection." We sat together in silence for a while.

I am reminded of a female client who worked with children. Her intention was to save them but she could not save herself. It was not allowed. The thing she feared most was her own power. In order to save herself she would have to experience herself as powerful and that was not a part of the formula she could allow.

When she was little her mother made her believe she was bad. Mother not only told her this but demonstrated it by putting her head in the oven and blaming my client. Mother said "You drove me to this". This made my client very powerful. She was so powerful that she could make her mother kill herself. So now she dares not to be openly powerful.

Her secret power maintains her belief that she is actually

bad. She must subordinate herself to others. She must let others decide for her. She can only try to please them and to keep them powerful, in order to save them from her.

She is, of course, sad and angry that her life is filled with sadness and anger. She knows it need not be like this, that it is not her fault, but she only knows it in her head, not in her heart.

She is so full up of this usual me, and so valuable is it, that to review its meaning in any way that makes a body rather than head difference, is an ongoing struggle for her.

Chapter Twelve

Preference and Commitment

State of art electric,
guaranteed by maker's guarantee.
Whooping caballeros
singing to their horses, one two three.
Gourmets sampling dinners,
Betters backing winners,
Paint on people's faces,
Gamblers pulling aces,
It's the land of desire.

Beautiful and ugly,
Who are you but what your eye beholds?
Is love satisfaction?
Wish that lead would turn to solid gold.
Flowers full of sweet scent,
Miners with their backs bent,
Blow up rubber playmates,
Body builders pumping weights,
It's the land of desire.

Mirroring reflections,
Is there a velocity of light?
Switching on the TV
Settle down and watch the latest fight.
Nuclear bomb objections,
Immortality injections,
Sex and drugs and implants,
Repeating mystic prayers and chants,
It's the land of desire.

Addiction is a scale which goes from mild preference to compulsion and obsession. We are all somewhere on this scale. A heroin addict once told me that his addiction was like sheltering in the wings of the angel of death, and very often that was the place he wanted to be.

His quest to be there was in some way the shadow of enlightenment in that his life was focussed and his mind one pointed. All that mattered was getting the next fix; everything else was subsumed to this goal.

Many on the so-called spiritual path make the same mistake, being goal oriented, attempting to transcend this life, covertly rubbishing it, denying the body and the mind. Rather than cherishing usual me, they attempt to destroy it.

Even if we were not able to be free of the karmic wheel, be one with the universe, and realise that all is spirit, the world would at least be on the path to being healed if we could cherish our humanity rather than try to destroy it. To try to make a better version of usual me is itself an act of violence.

Usual thinking is discrimination. I prefer this and I reject that. I feel comfortable in the clothes I wear; to wear a dress would be a challenge for me.

My clothes, my hairstyle, the food I eat, the books I read, the sex I enjoy, the films I watch, the furniture I buy, the way I decorate my house, the car I drive, the games I play; these are ways of usual me reminding usual me who Geoffrey is, the security blanket of consistency and character, a barrier against being temporary.

Geoffrey is totally attached to Geoffreyness. A measurable identity is needed to be able to act, but towards the compulsive/obsessive end of the spectrum, this attachment can interfere with my life and others' lives in harmful ways.

We are all addicted to something as a way of dealing with our lives, our successes and our disappointments. As if it were a separate entity, the coping behaviour, event or object seduces me, promising to fulfil my desires. The Devil tempts me with whatever is in my heart.

The strategies addicts adopt are a result of the disintegrated person's desire to return to the original situation and right the wrong. The underlying addiction is to the cycle as the person loses sight of the real desire, to regain integrity, and compulsively gathers evidence to prove that they are as degraded as they believe themselves to be. At least they get to be right.

Preference is to do with desire, what I want and what I do not want. The question is not whether or what I desire, but how I learn what to desire. It could be my religious upbringing that informs me about what is ok and not ok, or it could be a sudden or gradual conversion to the "Truth". It could be big business that constantly finds new ways to seduce us into believing it about what the objects of desire are, and how they will improve our lives. Those with money, and those who can borrow money, are in a feeding frenzy, consuming mass luxury, while others starve for food.

Acting out of commitment is to do with my word. This is the power I have to make agreements and do my best to make something happen because I said so. If it works, I am happy, if it doesn't, I want to know I did my best.

Usual me chooses vanilla ice cream out of preference, but can I hear the questions that life is asking of me? How willing is usual me to follow the task that life sets me and to answer the questions as truthfully as usual me can?

My answers to life's questions are in what usual me actually does, that is my dialogue, my little dance with life. We affect each other. Life affects usual me as it questions me, and usual me affects life with responses.

Therapy, like life, is an art. This is not to glorify or deify therapy, but why imagine that the theory of any art is any more than that: theory? Therapy books contain interesting information that has little to do with the practice of therapy. They inform us about our need to understand, our need to have ways of describing how and why humans beings are like they are and do what they do, that makes some kind of sense to the kind of people we believe we are and want to be.

Acting out of preference is the desiring part, the usual me that experiences the manifestations as the ten thousand things.

Acting out of commitment is desireless, the true me that is the mystery that usual me can never know.

◈

Chapter Thirteen • Death

It's the need for a saviour
It's the need to believe
In something or nothing
To pass the time 'til we leave

We humans can be special in lots of different ways. I want something, or the absence of something, because I am so special: The best of the worst, the worst of the best, the best of the best, the worst of the worst, the most or least average.

Being different is a big one. To be different, not one of the herd, is a highly desired state. This is vanity in action, the rise of usual me. Neither the world nor usual me is the initiator or the counter. I want to believe in mutually arising, but my desiring usual me has to be separate from the world to continue. That is the illusion. Then usual me can play all the attachment-separation games.

If usual me did not exist, difference and sameness would not exist. All the pushing and pulling and trying and giving up would also not exist.

What do I think about all day? What is the content of usual me mind? Usual me. True me is when usual me's quacking on about this and yapping on about that, which upholds the usual me world and my place in it, is over.

At first real is real, it is not an issue. Then real becomes an issue and the world is a dream. Then the world is real in the sense of being an expression of oneness, a faint mirror image of the whole. In some ways this other place is not attractive as it is a place that is not a place, a place without meaning. Usual me says "I will visit it often enough to understand it and discover its meaning".

I am real, then I am dreaming the world, then I am the dreamed, then I am real, then I am dreaming the world, then I am the dreamed, and so it goes. Usually only the language of usual me has been spoken, only the interpretation of usual me has been allowed.

As contracted usual me disappears, I am expanded true me. This is not an experience born of memory. Part of the expansion contraction cycle does not have a usual me in it. Getting usual me to be ok with this is not easy. To suicidal people complete absence of me can be a very attractive proposition, but that is not what I mean.

Death is a part of this, my death, not the nominalization. Usual me cannot be vain when death is real.

I first came into contact with dead people when I was part of the Jewish burial ritual. It knocked some of my self importance and arrogance out of me, but even death did not manage to make it permanent. I was in my early twenties living in Southport, a provincial Victorian sea-side town with a thriving Jewish community.

My father was the local kosher butcher and so we lived semi- publicly. The butcher shop was one of the focal points of Jewish life. People shopped there but also met and gossiped and argued.

I was invited to join the Chevra Kadisha, holy friends,

by my first major non-family mentor, Reverend Moshe Glazier. This was the burial society, a small number of men that could be called on to perform the Jewish ritual of cleaning and dressing the dead body.

Up to the age of about 14 or 15, I would go to his house every Friday night after dinner. I remember the dark winter evenings the best. I would arrive wrapped in the cold damp outside, and was instantly greeted by a huge coal fire roaring at me from the grate.

Twelve white candles, in two brass candelabras, were burning on the dining table which was covered with a white tablecloth, an open Bible ready. The temperature must have been over 100 Fahrenheit. It smelled like the Sabbath, a combination of the fire, the candles, and cinnamon biscuits, ginger cake, sweet red kosher wine and musty tradition.

We would sit at the table while his wife Kitty and her sister, Rae, sat in chintzy armchairs that were too big for them. The material was shiny from use. They would half listen and argue with each other as if I wasn't there. Rev. Glazier would say "Ok, let's learn." We would read that week's portion of the Bible in Hebrew then in English, trying to discover the meaning. This was my first brush with a search for meaning, and apparent nit-picking of words.

So it was he that invited me to join this exclusive group. He said to come along, to stay near the door and if I didn't like it, to leave and no-one would mention it again. I agreed, not really knowing what I was agreeing to, but I was young.

One evening I got a phone call. Can you be at the cemetery at 7.30? So with fear in my heart, and morbid curiosity driving me, I went to the cemetery. It was perfect evening for my initiation. Everything was covered in new snow that shone and sparkled with a yellow hue from the street lights.

The night was still and the rows of gravestones stood like

black dominos sprinkled with stardust, dark shadows angling across them. I knew someone has already arrived because of the footprints that made a path for me to a little part brick house that stood at one end of the Jewish section of the graveyard. I walked the path treading in the footprints as I went. I knocked. Later, when I was more experienced, I would just walk in.

Moshe Glazier was there, as was Sydney Galkoff who took over leadership when Glazier retired, but my eyes were irresistibly focused on the raised marble slab in the centre of the room. On the slab was a body wrapped in a white sheet. There was a small heater blowing in the corner.

My hand was shaken by each man as they arrived. There was also a direct look into my eyes. I felt frightened, excited, and expectant. My mouth was dry. I was light-headed. There was a slight buzzing in my ears. I could not concentrate on what people were saying to me.

All that mattered was that I was in the presence of death. There was a reverential, respectful, feel to the room. I was in an altered state, the first of many. I was a witness that first night, as every night I was there, a witness to the finality of death.

There was no doubt in my mind that the man who lay on the slab was dead. I could feel there was something missing. I knew from that moment on that Geoffrey was temporary on this Earth. This is something I forget a lot.

This could be the last thing I ever do. I might never leave this room. One day or night I too will do the last thing I will ever do, Geoffrey will breathe out and never breathe in again, his eyes will cease to see, his ears will cease to hear, his smell and taste will turn off, his brain will stop, his body will stop sensing and feeling and thinking. All the rhythms and beats and pulses will stop.

If I am going to die in the now why not live here? Usual me's reasoning is that if I practice being in the here and now and get used it, then when I am actually dying it will somehow be easier for usual me to bear, that I will be able to identify with the true mind that does not die: usual me is forever selfish.

This is one of the reasons I meditate. The actuality of my death somehow makes my life actual. It is a strange paradox; the finality of death gives my life vividness and intensity. How wondrous, how improbable to be here at all.

Chapter Fourteen

Singing the Glory of Forms

How much desire to kindle a Buddha?
How many sinners to balance the sainted?
How many haters to resurrect Jesus?
Oh how the pure promenade with the tainted.

True me and usual me are separated and connected by language, a word, a name, a noun, a verb, the smallest particle imaginable, the space between this and that. Both of these worlds are extraordinary, but the usual world appears ordinary by familiarity.

How magical it is to be able to speak and for another to understand the noises I make. How amazing to be able to decipher marks and to make meanings from them that we can share. How miraculous that this is at all. How tragic what we do with it.

Krishnamurti on what he called meditation,

"If you set out to meditate, it will not be meditation. If you set out to be good, goodness will never flower. If you cultivate humility, it ceases to be. Meditation is the breeze that comes in when you leave the window open; but if you deliberately keep it open, deliberately invite it to come, it will never appear."

This is a debate among some therapists: Is it possible, or desirable to invite true me to appear? Sounds like summoning up a spirit with a ritual. This is something I am averse to. I know the power of daily practice from learning a musical instrument and from meditating, but there is something about ritual that repels me.

It is like old dark magic that is on the obsessive side. It gets caught up with its own importance and become heavy and rule bound, up its own bum. I prefer a lighter model, laughing at our humanness, the tragedy and absurdity of being human.

I remember in a supervision group I was describing how I had been laughing at a client. I was asked if I meant laughing with, but sometimes we need to be laughed at and to laugh at ourselves to break the spell. This alleviates, a little, the painful realisation of the awful construction of our social world, the arena of usual mes, and how that has become our prison. Rebirth does not have to be painful, the usual me can laugh as well as cry.

So it is about opening the window naturally rather than deliberately, the opening, not the opener. It is like the student in Zen and the Art of Archery, not looking at the bull's-eye, just releasing the arrow. I think this is what Werner Erhard meant when he said,

"If you keep saying it the way it really is, eventually your word is law in the universe."

Nothing begets existence, and the ten thousand things

mutually arise with desire, can I be aware of both worlds? The true me looks on the usual me, sees it, knows it in its entirety, all in one go. Each is implicit in the other.

> As Kabir's beautiful song goes,
>
> "There is a strange tree, which stands without roots and bears fruit without blossoming;
> It has no branches and no leaves, it is lotus all over.
> Two birds sing there; one is the Guru
> And the other is the disciple:
> The disciple chooses the manifold fruits of life,
> And tastes them,
> And the Guru beholds in joy.
> What Kabir says is hard to understand:
> "The bird is beyond seeking, yet it is most clearly visible.
> The Formless is in the midst of all forms. I sing the glory of forms."

In singing the glory of forms, Kabir is also singing the glory of the formless, but nothing can be said about the formless, it is beyond words, beyond seeking. Formed, it is most clearly visible. In this sense, there is no need to summon true me, it is already here, implicit in the usual me, as the usual me is implicit in the true me.

As Lao Tsu said, these two are one, differing only in name. So when I sing the glory of forms, I am opening the window, not to let true me in, but to sing the glory of the opener, the window, the opening, the entering breeze, the wonder of the subject and the object, the marvellous mutuality of true me and usual me.

This is the secret of non attachment, that any object of

desire is a signpost to the formlessness from which it is formed. That is what we really want.

Most of my days are made of small things, sweeping the floor and washing up, baking bread, my five year old grandson singing me "Happy Birthday", catching the train, coffee in a polystyrene cup. Every now and again a so called big thing happens. If I can enjoy the small things, which when added together make up most of my life, then life is my vocation.

We have been tamed and domesticated from the moment we were born and this includes religious indoctrination.

The mystic, however, is a bit mad. The mystic does not kill others to save them. The mystic approach is a scientific approach. The mystic does not take things on faith or believe that something is true because tradition dictates. The mystic relies on practice and evidence gathered, not the authority of a priest or expert who has a hot line to God and is the interpreter of the holy books. There appears to be different ways of understanding this.

The story of Hui Neng, an early Zen hero. In the monastery the master asked for a poem to be written that would illustrate Zen in order to find his successor. Here is the chief disciple's,

> "Our body is the Bhodi tree,
> And our mind a mirror bright,
> Carefully wipe them hour by hour
> And let no dust alight."

Hui Neng was an illiterate country bumpkin who had listened to a priest reading Buddha's "Diamond Sutra" and been turned on by it. He had got a job in the kitchens at the Zen monastery. Someone read Hui Neng the poem. He got them to write down his poem. It read,

"There is no Bhodi tree
Nor stand of mirror bright.
Since all is void,
Where can dust alight?"

The first metaphor is that the mind is a mirror, but it can be a distorted by experience. It needs to be worked on regularly. Dust of any kind must be removed. A process and a structure are needed to do this work.

The other is also a metaphor, but one of nothingness. Nothing exists, not a negative nothing but a nothing full of potential. This kind of truth is harder to bear. We comfort ourselves with religious, humanistic and other beliefs.

We demand arbiters so we can know how to be, what to think, and how to behave. Awareness of self is the basic duality. I contract from being whole by separating into usual mes. This is the creation of the ten thousand usual mes which is the education process we all go through as we learn the current rules of society.

So are we aiming for true me which has no self relationship? This is impossible for usual me to imagine. In the second poem, none of that matters. Everything is void. All is one and therefore nothing because there is no other with which to compare it.

This sounds like a negative approach. The void and meaninglessness are not happy sounding ideas. But what I do have is the freedom to experience life in the way that I choose. The fact is I am here. My back is aching today. I have to deal with it. Old age is the price I pay for being alive. It is not personal.

I can be a victim of my body or accept and cherish it. If the universe had some predetermined meaning, I would not have the freedom to make my own. That is my freedom, to have a sense of self, to be aware of myself as another. With our sense of self we provide otherness to the universe.

The ability to self reflect is a blessing and a curse. We all intuit this. In the Genesis Bible story Adam and Eve were evicted from paradise when they became self aware after eating the fruit of the knowledge of good and evil, awareness of duality, fragmentation.

God was afraid that they would become like gods and, as usual, was not able to take any competition, especially that these jumped up humans would become immortal by eating of the tree of life.

I look around me, I have a name for everything I see, and any holes in my experience are quickly explained away as aberrations. The preferences with which I surround myself for familiarity, which I interpret as security, dull me to the expanded world, and so I am cocooned in a prison of my own making.

Do I feel the real wind on my face, a real pain in my heart, a real upsurge of love? What can I compare it to? It is like when I get my ears syringed and I suddenly I realise how little I was hearing before. And yet, because I can name most of this stuff; love, the table, the ceiling, some feelings, the Geoffrey, I act as if I do know something, whereas most of what I know consists of better, more sophisticated tricks, such as presenting workshops, driving a car, surfing the internet, allowing myself to be tamed by society for personal gain, and denying the suffering that most of the human race endures daily.

It is my experience of me that separates me from you. I am the source of my experience and I feel it with my body.

This sounds so strange, saying that experience distances me from you, but when I am aware that I experience you prejudicially as a collection of qualities, e.g. short, thin, white, female, homosexual, clever, happy, suffering, starving, religious, etc. we can be together in our humanity, cherishing the usual me we share, laughing at the layers of labels obscuring us from each other, connecting us to each other.

This is not about amputation. Cutting bits off me in an attempt to be whole is the process of fragmentation. Usual me is prejudicial, that will not change, it is a part of usual me's job description. What I can do is witness the process, feel the suchness of it.

Karma is the ultimate mortgage company and its customers are usual mes. "Reduce your monthly outgoings! Consolidate your debts (sins) in one handy package! Don't worry that your debt is eternal."

As long as fragmented usual me is in charge you can never repay your debt. Do not try to grow into something better or more. That effort is karma which means action. You as you are is enough. That's it. Nothing fancy or smart. No esoteric techniques. No special prayers. No special relationship with God.

The biggest and only change you will ever have to make is to cherish you as you are right now, all of you, full spectrum, the light and the shadow and all the colours in between.

I remember a young woman who I worked with some years ago. My interpretation of how well the therapy had gone was to do with how well I believed she had worked through various feelings about her brother.

Several months after the therapy, she wrote to me. She thanked me and said what had made the difference in how she felt about herself as a person, were the recipes I had printed out for her.

What had happened was that my wife has discovered she was lactose intolerant. At the same time I discovered that my client was also lactose intolerant. While I was printing out recipes from the internet for my wife, I printed out some for her too.

What had moved her was not any brilliant technique; it was just the human thing to do. That is what made the difference, her knowing that she was a person to me. That was never said with words.

The language of intimacy is a silent language. It co-exists with prejudicial, usual me language, and is often hidden, avoided, unknown. It is silent in the sense that is formless and so elastic. It ebbs and flows, it fills and empties.

How willing am I to end all the ways I hurt myself and you with all the reasons known and hidden? Do I miss living by sublimating desire, not being willing to recognise that a part of usual me is "Like a one eyed cat peeping in a sea food store"?

I do not mean allowing the id energy of usual me free reign, but what is repressed will surface if unacknowledged. Talking about change is easy; making plans to change at some point safely in the future that will never arrive. Sometimes someone says that they did something and then says "It wasn't me at all." Well, who was it then?

What is in me is me, even if it was alien to begin with. Most of what is "in me" was not mine to begin with. Keeping it going turns it into me. Yet what has become me, the usual me, is my vehicle to move through this life. It is the only tool I have got.

A mirror reflects whatever is in front of it. This means that I, as mirror, reflect the debris of experience, and that debris is usual me. I can wipe usual me off the mirror, get that there is no dust, no mirror, no wiper, or sing the glory of form by cherishing the dust, the mirror, and the reflecting; "beholding in joy." For me that is being spiritual. You pays your money and you takes your choice.

◆

Chapter Fifteen • Believing

Belief:
The Sun revolves around the Earth
Belief:
The Earth revolves around the Sun
Belief:
The Sun revolves
Belief:
The Earth revolves
Belief:
The Sun
Belief:
The Earth
Belief:
God loves us
Belief:
God, loves, us.

What is reality? A fiction that lasted long enough to solidify? Is there something out there apart from usual me? Is there any outside to this? It is important to usual me that I believe my experience of the world. All sorts of things could happen if the world and usual me's spin on it somehow separate.

The world in which we live is the one we believe in. All the wrangling and fighting, all the violence, is born and nurtured with belief. Usual me is the believer and the unbeliever, the believed and the unbelieved. Stop, look around, listen, this is the world we all live in. We all know what is going on. We all feel it.

Some of us can dissociate enough to deny the reality for most people on this planet. The depressive and manic symptoms we are expressing are the manifestation of human suffering, all of it. We are one entity. When one suffers, we all suffer. We each create our part and subscribe to the whole. That subscription is non voluntary.

We could do this in a way which is respectful. By this I mean waking up to the disgraceful way we treat each other. It is time to stop pretending.

It is not important whether we are good or bad or free or anything, that is just avoidance. It is what we are doing and allowing to be done. Usual me rules all this with belief. People are dying from hunger right now. People are torturing and killing each other right now out of sectarian political and religious beliefs.

This is not about changing beliefs; it is about recognising the obvious. For usual me that recognition is transformational.

We can stand up and be counted. We can make a difference. The human being entity is sick, but suffering does not have to be the law. We can heal ourselves by healing how we are with each other. We do not have to suffer any more. If there ever was a lesson to learn in suffering, let's learn it and move on.

This is the next evolutionary jump, a jump heralded by thinking in words and pictures. Thinking in words and pictures has migrated out of our fantasies into the physical reality. We live our lives in our words and pictures, a virtual world where symbols and actuality are blurred. Symbols have become highly prized; some of us are willing to kill and to be killed for a symbol. Many of us have lived and died horribly because of a symbol, because of belief.

So what sort of words and pictures are we living in now? This is no secret. This era has nearly run its course, as the status quo breaks down, chaos emerges, and once again we are in a cusp straddling the old and the new.

There are other things to believe in. The collective dream of usual me has been exciting and dramatic but violence has had its day. It is enough. It is time. We could dream a new dream, a dream in which being is the context, where we do the right thing.

We could choose an elegant route, a dream of consciousness that does not include usual me vanity or karma. We either annihilate ourselves through war, starvation and disease, or we honour our embodiment and move out into the universe in love. It's like leaving the nest and all that movement implies.

The territorial aspect of usual me is appalled by this. What about all my possessions, including my body? What about me, what about Geoffreyness? It is all very well talking about sharing, but this is my house, my car, my job, my relationship, my reputation.

Usual me does not want to share all of this. If usual me is feeling generous, I will sometimes share a portion of my surplus, but my position and my stuff is mine.

The thing is usual me, Geoffrey, is a conglomeration of fragments and is not whole, is not perfect, and never will be. Usual me can fiddle around with itself for millennia, analysing, trying, working hard to improve, but none of that will ever go beyond the cosmetic. I am referring to a contextual change, a shift in consciousness.

Change is not accumulative, bit by bit by bit. Change

happens out of time, all of a sudden. It is like experiencing experience. This does not make sense, and that is the point, anything that makes sense will not do that particular trick.

I am speaking of the notion of critical mass. If reality is a description, an agreement, then when enough usual mes agree that enough is enough, and critical mass is reached, we will transform peacefully and gracefully into the next episode of our journey of imagination as energy beings across the universe.

◆

Bibliography

Lenny Bruce (1975) how to talk dirty and influence people. Granada Publishing. London. Various recordings.

Martin Buber (1996) I and Thou. Translated Ronald Gregor Smith. T & T Clark. Edinburgh.

Buddha The Diamond Sutra. Translated A.F. Price. http://community.palouse.net/lotus/diamond1-5.htm

Charles Calhoun (Jesse Stone) (1954) Shake Rattle and Roll performed by Big Joe Turner. Unichappell Music (BMI). Atlantic Records. (I'm like a one eyed cat....)

Carlos Castaneda see website for books DVDs etc. www.castaneda.org

Ram Dass (1976) Grist for the Mill. Wildwood House. London

Bob Dylan, (1965) Highway 61 Revisited. Audio. CBS. USA. Renewed 1993 Special Rider Music

Werner Erhard (1978) Biography by William Warren Bartley 111. Clarkson and Potter. New York. Also www.wernererhard.com

Viktor E Frankl (2004) Man's Search for Meaning. Rider and Co.

Václav Havel (1986) "Dear Dr. Husák" Václav Havel or Living in Truth, edited by Jan Vladislav Faber & Faber, London "Dear Dr. Husák" (April 1975), addressed to Dr. Gustav Husák, who was then the general secretary of the Czechoslovak Communist Party, is Havel's first major public statement after being blacklisted in 1969. The letter was first published in English, in this translation, in Encounter (September 1975).

Eugene Herrigel (1988) Zen in the Art of Archery. Arkana.

WJ Johnson (1994) Bhagavad Gita Oxford University Press

Kabir (1995) Songs of Kabir translated by Rabindranith Tagore. Samuel Weiser. York Beach, Maine.

Jiddu Krishnamurti (1980) Meditations. Gollancz. London

LaoTsu (Laotze) (1902) The Book of the Simple Way (Tao-Teh-King) translated by Walter Gorn Old. Philip Wellby, London. (1973) Tao Teh Ching translation by Gia-Fu Feng and Jane English. Wildwood House, Middlesex.

Hui Neng http://buddhism.about.com/od/zen/a/Zen4.htm

Monty Python (1983) The Meaning of Life. DVD. Celandine Films. Universal Studios.

Joan Riviere (1952) On the Genesis of Psychical Conflict in Earliest Infancy in Developments in Psycho-Analysis. M. Klein, P. Heiman, S. Isaacs, J. Riviere, eds. Hogarth. London

Ken Wilber (1998) The Essential Ken Wilber, Shambhala. USA.

Robert M. Young Selected Papers and Articles. www.human-nature.com/rmyoung/papers

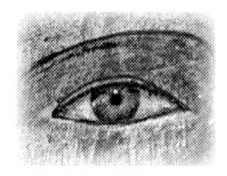

Contacting the Author

Geoffrey can be contacted via his website:
www.heartandmind.co.uk

Index

Abraham 20
actualisation 18, 25
actualised 14, 25, 34

body 12, 17, 25, 28, 42, 43, 56,
    61, 73, 75, 80, 81, 86,
    87, 88, 93
boundaries 8, 25, 59
Bruce, Lenny 20, 96
Buber, Martin 13, 96
Buddha 22, 83, 96

Castaneda, Carlos 40, 96
causal 12
celebrity 30, 33

death 5, 15, 20, 23, 25, 27, 28,
    31, 32, 33, 46, 75, 78,
    79, 81, 82
duality 12, 87, 88
Dylan, Bob 20, 96

energy 16, 19, 27, 29, 36, 49,
    61, 90, 94
enlightenment 23, 25, 31, 75
Erhard, Werner 6, 7, 54, 58

Frankl, Victor 26, 28, 96
freedom 33, 34, 48, 87

Genesis 88, 97
God 19, 20, 21, 22, 24, 29, 33,
    58, 86, 88, 89, 91
growth 17, 18, 31, 102

Havel, V 32, 33, 97
humanity 9, 43, 75, 88
humour 23

identity 12, 20, 24, 29, 76
imagination 36, 60, 66, 94
individual 19, 20, 23, 24, 25,
    26, 31, 38, 40
intention 34, 36, 72
intimacy 9, 13, 16, 42, 45, 59,
    62, 64, 66, 67, 71, 72

Jesus 20, 83

Kabir 58, 85, 97
Karma 89
Krishna 21
Krishnamurti 83, 97

Lao Tsu 42, 85
love 7, 11, 16, 17, 21, 27, 29,
    44, 45, 46, 47, 58, 67,
    68, 74, 88, 93

meaning 15, 17, 19, 21, 23,
    24, 26, 46, 51, 67, 73,
    79, 80, 87, 96, 97
mirror 10, 30, 37, 43, 79, 86,
    87, 90
money 70, 76, 90
myth 46, 66

otherness 9, 13, 88

paranoia 42, 43
parts 12, 28, 49, 57, 71, 72
process 9, 25, 36, 42, 43, 44,
    58, 62, 63, 87, 89
psychology 58
Python, Monty 97

quacking 14, 78

reality 8, 16, 21, 25, 27, 31,
    36, 38, 40, 41, 46, 52,
    53, 64, 91, 92, 94
reflections 10, 75
religion 19, 20

self 9, 14, 18, 19, 23, 24, 25,
    29, 32, 34, 39, 42, 52,
    55, 68, 79, 87, 88, 102
silence 32, 36, 69, 72

soul 10, 17, 31
special 18, 19, 23, 33, 57, 78,
    89
spiritual 9, 17, 65, 75, 90, 102
subtle 12
survival 12, 14, 15, 28, 46, 56

truth 8, 31, 76, 87, 97

violence 21, 28, 29, 33, 34, 75,
    92, 93

Wilber, Ken 97
wounds 30, 40

Zen 84, 86, 97

PS AVALON PUBLISHING

About PS Avalon

PS Avalon Publishing is an independent and committed publisher offering a complete publishing service, including editorial, manuscript preparation, printing, promotion, marketing and distribution. As a small publisher enabled to take full advantage of the latest technological advances, PS Avalon Publishing can offer an alternative route for aspiring authors working in our particular fields of interest.

As well as publishing, we offer a comprehensive education programme including courses, seminars, group retreats, and other opportunities for personal and spiritual growth. Whilst the nature of our work means we engage with people from all around the world, we are based in Glastonbury which is in the West Country of England.

new poetry books

Our purpose is to bring you the best new poetry with a psychospiritual content. Our intent is to make poetry relevant again, offering work that is contemplative and inspirational, with a dark, challenging edge.

self development books

We publish inspiring reading material aimed at enhancing your life development without overburdening you with too many words. Everything is kept as simple and as accessible as possible.

journals

With its full colour design, easy on-line availability, and most of all with its exciting and inspiring contents, *The Synthesist* journal is a popular offering to the psychospiritual world and beyond.

PS AVALON PUBLISHING
Box 1865, Glastonbury,
Somerset BA6 8YR, U.K.

www.psavalon.com

info@psavalon.com